PRAISE FOR *HAIRCUTS BY CHILDREN*

'This is one of the most significant books about children I have read in years. In detailing his vital and exhilarating work with his performance company, Mammalian Diving Reflex, Darren O'Donnell documents how he and his collaborators have experimented in reframing basic tenets of the adult-child social contract – to fantastic results. I will be watching eagerly to see what they do next.'
— Amy Fusselman, author of *Savage Park: A Meditation on Play, Space, and Risk for Americans Who Are Nervous, Distracted, and Afraid to Die*

'A surprising analysis by performance artist Darren O'Donnell about the roles children play in making the adult world, and how they can be a springboard for social change.'
— Kio Stark, author of *When Strangers Meet: How People You Don't Know Can Transform You*

'This tremendous, important book highlights the negative effects of our current concept of childhood on all aspects of society, imposing powerlessness, marginalizing "child-like" aspects of the human condition, and, as Darren suggests, only enabling adults to take one of two roles in relation to children: authoritarian or anarchist. He throws down the gauntlet to the cultural sector as being the natural arena to start the revolution that could radically change our lives for the better.'
— Susan Sheddan, Tate Learning

Haircuts by Children and Other Evidence for a New Social Contract

Darren O'Donnell

Coach House Books, Toronto

first edition

Published with the generous assistance of the Canada Council for the Arts and the Ontario Arts Council. Coach House Books also gratefully acknowledges the support of the Government of Canada through the Canada Book Fund and the Government of Ontario through the Ontario Book Publishing Tax Credit.

LIBRARY AND ARCHIVES CANADA CATALOGUING IN PUBLICATION

O'Donnell, Darren, 1965-, author
    Haircuts by children : and other evidence for a new social contract / Darren O'Donnell.

Issued in print and electronic formats.
ISBN 978-1-55245-337-7 (paperback).--ISBN 978-1-77056-479-4 (mobi).--
ISBN 978-1-77056-478-7 (pdf).--ISBN 978-1-77056-477-0 (epub)

    1. Social contract. 2. Cultural industries. 3. Children's rights. 4. Children--Social conditions. 5. Children--Economic conditions. I. Title.

PS8579.D64H34 2016   C814'.6   C2016-904396-7

Haircuts by Children is available as an ebook: ISBN 978 1 77056 477 0 (EPUB), ISBN 978 1 77056 478 7 (PDF).

Purchase of the print version of this book entitles you to a free digital copy. To claim your ebook of this title, please email sales@chbooks.com with proof of purchase. (Coach House Books reserves the right to terminate the free download offer at any time.)

This book is dedicated, first and foremost, to Sanjay Ratnan, who had the guts to message me and meet with me at Burger King, back in 2010 when he was just fourteen.

It's also dedicated to the crew of young people – now not so young – I have worked with since then and with whom I've had some of the best times of my life: Kathy Vuu, Chozin Tenzin, Chosang Tenzin, Isabel Ahat, Ahash Jeeva, Dana Liu, Nerupa Somasale, Virginia Antonipillai, Kiam Lam-Bellissimo, Ngawang Luding, Wendell Williams, and Thipeeshan Bala.

A further dedication goes out to Eva Verity, my Mammalian partner, who assumed her senior position in the company when, at twenty-seven years old, she was close to a kid herself. None of this would have happened without her vision and hard work – she has kept the company alive.

Finally, to Alice Fleming, who sorted me out, propped me up, got me back on track, and without whom this book would have never been finished.

I love you all and consider you the best of friends.

CONTENTS

PREFACE

Working with children was never the plan. In fact, for the bulk of my twenty-five-year career as artistic director of performance company Mammalian Diving Reflex, I created work that was not particularly child-friendly: a musical about the fictional assassination of philosopher Jacques Lacan; a monologue claiming that psychosis, if integrated properly, bore a stronger resemblance to spirituality than insanity; a monologue expressing empathy for the 9/11 perpetrators' desire to get on a fast track to heaven (in which I had an emotional discussion with a frightened streetcar); and a couple of live cartoons, one featuring two white-furred mice screaming at each other about racism; the other about a scientist and his clone, both with boxes stuck on their heads, trying unsuccessfully to conceive a baby, complete with songs. My work was edgy, experimental, provocative, and – most importantly – ridiculously playful.

Haircuts by Children was, in its way, typical of what Mammalian had always done: a bunch of little kids were *very briefly* trained, then paid to work in a hair salon, their inexperienced hands wielding scissors very near to adult eyes, as they distributed some of the most hilarious hairstyles ever created. I first presented *Haircuts by Children* in 2006, and the work is still edgy, experimental, provocative, and ridiculously playful. But it's also something else. The chaos the project triggered in salons was a new experience for me, a performance where new ways of being together with children materialized and created a familial vibe amongst a bunch of strangers. This came as an unsettling surprise, and I returned home after each of the first four Toronto performances with an overwhelming feeling of loneliness. Perhaps, at forty, my biological clock was finally kicking in. But I still had no desire to actually have children – I was too busy, too single, too selfish. I just wanted to make art with them; collaborating with these kids had been way more enjoyable than with any of the adults I'd ever worked with.

So I started to work with kids – a lot! Collaborations with children forced their way into my life and career, becoming my primary focus, to the exclusion of almost everything else. While it might seem like kids' stuff, in reality, learning to create art with children that entertained an adult audience – while also challenging the accepted role of children in the world – turned out to be more provocative than inviting audience members onstage to make out with me at the climax of *A Suicide Site Guide to the City* or threatening to kill every single white person in the audience of *White Mice*.

More than simply some good fun with the kids, *Haircuts by Children* is a project that models an aesthetic of civic engagement. I'd just written a book to tease out what such an aesthetic might mean: *Social Acupuncture* (2006) focused on how to build social intelligence through the triggering of discomfort between real people in real situations, using the institutions of civil society and the people that populate them as material in an artistic practice. Performance – acting almost as a magical cloak of invisibility – allows for the disallowed, by naming it 'art.' How else could we get away with children running a salon and inflicting insane haircuts on the public? In *Social Acupuncture*, I concluded that an understanding of the aesthetic should be counterposed to its exact opposite: the anesthetic. I was searching for an approach to civic engagement that struggles against the dull numbness of what has become of much activist art – something charged with legitimate feeling, not to mention a good deal of fun. Kids, it turns out, are good at experiencing feelings and having fun.

The inclusion of children in Mammalian as central to my artistic practice has radically altered my life, and I wrote this book hoping I can convince others to try it out, perhaps radically altering their lives too. These changes in my life have, among other effects, made me understand children and childhood in a very different way. I've come to strongly believe that children deserve a new social contract, one that adjusts their position as the last visible minority we can still legally discriminate against, toward one that not only invites their participation in all things affecting them, but that can position them as leaders, applying their particular childish codes of morality and ethics – not just for their sake, but for everyone's.

1

CHILDREN VS. CAPITALISM

I consider myself an embarrassed revolutionary, hoping for rapid, wide-scale social change toward higher levels of equity and fairness. I don't think it's too much to ask; I just want to live in a world where everyone has enough and no one has way too much. I'm embarrassed because not only is wide-scale social change toward fairness exactly what is not happening, things are actually swinging in the other direction, with increasing momentum, and maintaining this hope feels, more and more, like idiotic naïveté. No one seems to have a new plan, or at least a new plan able to galvanize critical mass, and none of the old plans seem to have worked out too well. The idea of tossing a wrench into the gears of capitalism just hasn't panned out, so maybe we need to rethink things and find something else to toss in. I'm thinking children.

I'm not the only one who thinks children should be playing a much bigger role in the world. Article 12 of the 1989 UN Convention on the Rights of the Child (UNCRC; Appendix 3) provides a basis for a way to think about young people as participants in the social order. It reads: 'States Parties shall assure to the child who is capable of forming his or her own views the right to express those views freely in all matters affecting the child.'

While 'expressing views' is a narrow way to describe participation, Article 12 has been taken up and commonly understood as protecting children's participation rights.[1] These rights should need protecting for all the reasons regularly cited when psychologists, social geographers, and legal scholars take up the topic, as they often do: for the young people to develop a sense of control, increased ability to handle stressful situations, enhanced trust in others, self-esteem, and the feeling of being respected, to enhance education and development, to learn how to respect others' views, and more.

But the reach of these rights is actually extensive: 'all matters affecting the child.' That's a pretty big list. It is hard to think of any important social or political institution, process, or system that doesn't affect young people: the market, the education system, the judicial system, the electoral system, the entertainment industry, the medical industry, almost all technology, and on and on. The list is almost endless, and can pretty much be summed up with one word: *everything*. Everything affects children – but it's bigger than the individual kids. I'm all for helping every child achieve her best potential, of course, but here I want to focus on the ways that increased participation of children and young people will make for a better society in general. There are advantages to all of us when children are among us. On a simple level, hanging out with kids encourages calm civility – after all, no one relishes the idea of having a yelling match in front of a crowd of four-year-olds – and children are expert at small joys, having a total mastery of play, an attribute many adults find challenging. Imagine if kids were almost always everywhere.

I am proposing the utopian idea that children should not be corralled off in some district of life known as childhood, where their contribution is – if allowed at all – limited. Children and young people should be folded much more into the decision-making processes that drive our society, the level of their participation read as a barometer of a given institution's commitment to human rights. Further, the increased participation of children across as many aspects of life as possible – but most importantly, the world of work – might be a stealthy way to smuggle in a little equity and fairness without triggering too many alarm bells. This is a vision of children as contributors of an expertise arising from their particular youthful capacities, an expertise that could change the game, yielding widespread social change and a realignment toward more equitable conditions for all. The effects on the systems we rely on might well be revolutionary – it could topple capitalism.

I know that sounds even more idiotic than sitting around and waiting for the revolution. But consider what the UN Committee on the Rights of the Child had to say in 2006 about that very modest question of the child's right to express his or her views:

Recognizing the right of the child to express views and to participate in various activities, according to her/his evolving capacities, is beneficial for the child, for the family, for the community, the school, the State, for democracy … The new and deeper meaning of this right is that *it should establish a new social contract* [my italics]. One by which children are fully recognized as rights-holders who are not only entitled to receive protection but also have the right to participate in all matters affecting them … This implies, in the long term, changes in political, social, institutional and cultural structures.[2]

The committee understands the implications of implementing the 1989 UNCRC: there will have to be some pretty big changes, extending well beyond the benefits to the individual child, changes that will affect everyone and everything. The idea that incorporating children more fully has the potential to challenge stubborn ideological deadlocks is supported by the fact that the UNCRC is so widely ratified, with all countries but the U.S. on board. That's a pretty impressive consensus. The presence of kids can help us agree on even difficult issues, a view the UNCRC advances, with the no-brainer that children have the potential to aid understanding among cultures and societies by approaching questions of morality and ethics in ways very different from adults. Someone's religion is not likely to cause anxiety when there's a game of tag to be played, and fairness – accepting equitable redistribution – is so totally logical to most children that they won't shut up about it.

I realize I'm taking a risk in proposing this idea, the same risk that anyone who does any kind of work with kids takes on and, in fact, the risk that children themselves constantly face: I may not be taken seriously. But being quickly dismissed is a bad reason to stop talking, thinking, and trying. When shifts in attitudes come, they can come fast, leaving the world utterly transformed. And it does need to be transformed. A change is required, if not a massive over-haul, in the way a capitalist system has concentrated wealth in an increasingly small and rarefied stratum of the social hierarchy. We need a change in who benefits from our social, economic, and political activities. Inequity is rising fast, and it is primed to look like nothing we've ever seen before.[3] Some futurists, like Dr. Oliver Curry, an evolutionary theoriest from the London School of Economics, even predict we're risking the evolution of two species – one tall, healthy, and wealthy and the other, short, dim-witted, and poor.

The left's pivot over the last thirty years toward a politics of identity has been blamed by some commentators for driving people apart and contributing to the recent rise of an extremist, racist, sexist, homophobic far right. But whether that's true or not, the politics of identity have not provided the tools to create a movement with enough mass to really get up in capitalism's ugly face. Judith Butler, a leading figure in challenging the gender binary in both academic and popular contexts, also has doubts about the efficacy of identity politics. She believes it 'fails to furnish a broader conception of what it means, politically, to live together across differences'[4] and she turns to the idea of precarity, or precariousness – living with no stable, reliable, and consistent employment – as a concept to rally around, a site of alliance.

And this is where the kids come in. If we're looking for a population with nearly infinite identities expressed by the individuals within it, all of whom share the condition of precarity, we don't have to look much further than children, even the richest of whom are denied many basic rights, including the right to work for money. Children are everywhere, all identity groups have them, and all of us, no matter our identity or our politics, have been a child and experienced the acute powerlessness that is the child's condition. Can the child – and efforts to infiltrate much of the world with the presence of children – provide a strategy for destabilizing the status quo? And if so, can this strategy attract the critical mass currently missing from the many fractured movements that wrestle with the question of fairness?

Our understanding of what it means to be a child and what children are capable of contributing is rapidly evolving. I believe we do have the possibility of both subverting business as usual and finding a common cause to organize around, a stealthy little cause that, at first, seems naive and innocuous – sure, let the kids in – but that might radically revolutionize the world. So let's get on with this revolution, let's parachute the little kids in everywhere, like tiny anarchic guerrillas, with the first question being, how do we get the whippersnappers back to work, one area where capitalism has particularly strong purchase?

In this book, I turn to recent developments in the arts and cultural sectors in which children and young people increasingly play important leadership roles. Working with kids to make financially viable, aesthetically successful art for the international performing arts market – as I do – is, admittedly, a narrow case study, but many of the benefits kids bring if fully included in this sector map fit neatly onto places where adults and children already interact: the family, school, extracurricular activities, online, and, oftentimes, the market. Some of the principles of our engagement with children in the arts can inform other pathways to including kids in the everyday institutions that make up our social fabric, our world. What happens when we put kids in boardrooms, in Silicon Valley, in our marketing and accounting departments, our parliaments, and our newsrooms?

Perhaps what's happening in arts and culture can be considered a pilot, a way to test and develop new methods of including the widespread participation of children across many other aspects of life, with the goal of evolving this new social contract, yielding changes in political, social, institutional, and cultural structures that will benefit the family, the community, the State, and democracy. In short: everything.

But first let's talk about the kids. Just what exactly are they? What do we mean when we say that someone is a child?

What it means to be a child, and what the capacities of a child are understood to be, are not historically fixed values. Our current social order, for the most part, views children as *becoming* and not *being*. Children, we tend to believe, are moving toward a destination: adulthood. They are constituted in opposition to adulthood, and considered to be in a state of preparation for taking on life's 'real' responsibilities once they are old enough, when they reach an age that is locked in law. They are on their way toward being finished. However, it is possible to conceive of young people not as headed toward a more perfected state, but as who they are right now, a view that prioritizes the young person's being at this moment over that of the adult they may eventually become. Accepting that their being is as legitimate as anyone else's would, ultimately, require recognizing that they do have a real stake in all discussions affecting them – and also that most issues really do affect them.

Shifting away from the psychology of development lays bare an uncomfortable fact: adults themselves hardly resemble the fully formed, rational entities that are popularly understood to be the province of adulthood. Beyond being 'grown-up' or just simply older, we really don't have much of a clue about, let alone a consensus on, what it means to be an adult. Certainly to be an adult is to be many, many things we think of as childlike: vulnerable, mistaken, confused, petulant, afraid, irrational, and despairing. We never stop making missteps, learning, and growing up. But that doesn't mean we don't sometimes have our shit mostly together. Just like many children do.

Feminist legal scholar Martha Albertson Fineman points out that prevailing political and legal theories assume that the universal or typical human subject is autonomous, self-sufficient, rational, and competent. It is this idea of the typical human for which laws are written – laws that, for the most part, do not apply to children, who are generally not legally responsible for their actions. Therefore, the universal human subject, around whom we understand human rights and which we consider the default, is an adult. Which is to say, not a child. Adulthood produces the category of childhood; the idea of the autonomy of adults makes no sense without the lack of autonomy implied in the idea of children. We've seen the shape of that universal subject change, however gradually or imperfectly, to accommodate greater rights for women, racialized people, and, increasingly, trans and other gender-variant folks. And we can likewise anticipate – if not actively work toward – the dissolution of the strict binary that is adult and child.

The first step is to stop assigning essential and unchanging qualities to either adults or children. Every adult and every child has the capacities and abilities they have: some adults are more childlike than others, some require the same care that a baby requires for their entire lives, and some children are, at a young age, resilient, rational, and independent. Practically speaking, the best, safest approach to breaking down this binary may be to err on the side of caution and assume that adults, as commonly understood, simply do not exist.

We are all children, we are all vulnerable, and we are all always figuring out how to cope with complex situations in ways that will be, in all likelihood, less than perfect. In the end, the notions of childhood and adulthood are stereotypes, with all the coercion that being a stereotype entails.[5] But beyond a stereotype, childhood is a way to relegate a big chunk of the population to the status of eternal other, less than and separate from the rest of us.

As a way to address this otherness, Fineman argues that we need to look more closely at vulnerability, which is 'universal and constant, inherent in the human condition.' She suggests we position vulnerability as central to what we think of as a typical person, contrasting it with the individual imagined in liberal political theory, where the 'typical' person is understood to be self-sufficient, rational, always personally responsible, and not particularly vulnerable.

Centring a vulnerable subject, like, say, a child, reveals some of the brokenness of a society 'conceived as constituted by self-interested individuals with the capacity to manipulate and manage their independently acquired and overlapping resources.'[6] Capitalism is absolutely reliant on the idea of this individual, a rational actor who trundles to the market every day to happily exchange their labour for a few dollars, the notion of the fairness of this arrangement hinging on this ideology of self-aware, rational self-sufficiency.

Fineman points to the idea of the vulnerable subject as a 'more accurate and complete universal figure to place at the heart of social policy.' Vulnerability is typically a condition that causes the state and other institutions to intervene in the social sphere, and using a framework of vulnerability opens things up to consider children the same way we consider adults. Imagine if vulnerability were central to our world view instead of a symbol of failure: it would become possible to shift the universal subject to include central aspects of the experience of children – which are also sure to be aspects of the adult experience. Within a vulnerability framework, every child is one of us and, as such, has the same right to participate in the world, and any systems not amenable to their participation – capitalism, say – would be considered unfair. If the universal or typical person – the vulnerable – has a hard time getting their act together to be of use to capitalism, then how useful, really, is capitalism?

'Are you expecting children to drive cars?' people often joke with me. But the thing is, in a few years, I don't expect anyone to be driving cars. The world is changing so rapidly that everything is up for grabs, really, with changes to the world of work and the production of value starting to reincorporate children in meaningful ways. In fact, children and young people have, in some respects, already secured sovereign realms – spaces in which they rule, where they call the shots, set the trends, generate the wealth, and make stuff happen. Mark Zuckerberg and his crew, for instance, are constantly chasing after the kids, attempting to harness and channel the little guys' interactions on Facebook and spinning it into wealth, and this trend is rising: think of YouTube superstars like Sabrina Cruz and Ben J. Pierce, both teens who cater their content entirely to younger audiences, or the ten-year-old kid from Quebec who goes by the name 'Sceneable' on YouTube. Sceneable has over forty thousand subscribers and well over two million views for his various video essays on the values of communism, the dangers of capitalism, and the compatibility of Christianity with homosexuality. The kid's a hardworking public intellectual. In this strange world, where many adults seem to prefer childlike things – witness the staggering popularity among grown-ups of colouring books, board games, Harry Potter, and *Twilight* movies – and where the rules are shifting under us, children suddenly have a new kind of power, one that is particularly pronounced in the realm of arts and culture, and could be expanded upon even more, extending to other areas, where it might end up changing the game.

I'm proposing to start my little revolution in arts and culture for a number of reasons, not the least of which is the sector's strong health. In the January 2016 Creative Industries Economic Estimates, the U.K.'s Department for Culture, Media and Sport reported that over the course of the last four years, the sector has been growing rapidly in the U.K. There is similar evidence in other areas of the world.[7] In addition to offering the excitement of being involved in a rapidly growing sector, inviting young people into a healthy industry fulfills an ethical obligation that any proposal like this must meet.

Beyond economic health, it's helpful that the consumption of arts and culture is everywhere. In some form or another, arts and culture are a regular part of most people's daily experience, a situation unimaginable even forty years ago. In a world where information and knowledge form the basis of much of the economy, one's ability to generate, build, wield, and trade on cultural capital is a constant backdrop in our lives. Aspects of artistic expression are now a big part of how we interact, communicate, and define ourselves – Instagram filters are an obvious example – as formerly professional-level technologies have become abundant, accessible, and easy to use. The arts have transcended the walls of the white cube, black box, or beige symphony hall and become a decentralized forum for bringing people together and getting them interacting in atypical and often more open ways. Cities are crawling with festivals of all sorts; galleries are constantly busting out participatory events; public talks, panels, and debates offer intellectual adventure; food is often the theme of participatory cultural activities; and crafting and design shows are ubiquitous – all engaging a population that has come to depend on the ingestion of arts and culture to provide life with meaning and connection. Arts and culture don't tend to close you off to the experience of others but rather facilitate openness and understanding. Cultural conversance is power, and we build our identities around it more than ever.

This new and unrivalled ubiquity is shared intergenerationally with children who are, increasingly, contributing members of our global culture and of global trends in the sector. This can be seen in publicly funded arts and cultural institutions, which always keep at least one eye on programming for young people and families; in commercial industries, which are well aware of the power of the consuming child, pursuing parents' wallets; and online, where children's role on the internet is large, influential, and here to stay. We can't ever slide back to a day before a shared global culture went crazy over the video meme *David After Dentist* – and many others like it – featuring a six-year-old kid high out of his mind after dental surgery,[8] which ended up providing an income for David and his family. Culture and kids, together at last, are here to stay.

As some of these ideas suggest, the fact that it is happening already is another reason for proposing arts and culture as a viable location for piloting an increase in youth participation in the world in general. Young people are engaged with the sector primarily as consumers but, more and more, also as content creators, trendsetters, and leaders. This is particularly the case in the realms of digital and social media, domains that overlap with and influence so much of the rest of our lives, completely and irrevocably intersecting with the body toward a freaky future of who-the-hell-can-say, other than the certainty that children and young people will continue to be front and centre.

Another, very practical, reason for locating this social experiment in the middle of arts and culture is the convenient fact that there are already provisions in labour law that allow children to work in some areas of the industry and systems in place to facilitate and even promote it. These provisions illustrate one way in which the arts get a bit of a pass, how they are socially sanctioned to make things happen that are a little out of the ordinary. Arts and culture comprise a magical sector that can bring populations together to marvel at ideas, believe in something, and sit with uncertainty in a way in which, in theory anyway, everyone is invited to take part.

My work with the youth I met through Mammalian Diving Reflex is clear proof that success might be found in thinking beyond after-school arts programs to keep kids off the street or to build confidence or other positive attributes. I'm talking about involving children in the viable production of cultural activities and products that are then circulated in contemporary arts markets to test this new way of being and working together with young people. Collaborating with children to create work for the 'real world' for 'real money' is a way to pilot and test the idea of the wider participation of young people in society as contributing members, and to see if their presence can bring the ideas of equity and fairness to the table.

Hauling cultural policy out of a neoliberal mind-set (where the focus is on cultural consumption) and into the promise of productive community-building is one vital task at hand; children are ideal collaborators in this. Public policy scholar Allen J. Scott, writing about creative participation in the urban civic sphere, points out that 'any push to achieve urban creativity in the absence of a wider concern for conviviality and camaraderie (which need to be distinguished from the mechanical conception of "diversity") in the urban community as a whole is doomed to remain radically unfinished.'[9] What better place to start a radical overhaul to empower a creative citizenry than with the children who share our neighbourhoods? And what better strategy than inviting those children in to take over our operations?

My examples of how radically children's engagement can alter an organization, making it better and stronger, are all drawn from my own experiences, including working with kids in festivals and art venues around the world – venues that often position themselves as critical friends to the democratic process and civil society. Such institutions place higher and higher value on civic engagement – sometimes willingly, sometimes to please funders. But, regardless of purity of motive, the ways in which these organizations interact with the social sphere produce not just projects about knowledge and ideas, but projects that trigger actual, real experiences between people as a function of the aesthetic. And that aesthetic experience can be surprising, even subversive. Working with children does not necessarily produce visions of sugarplum fairies, adorably awkward performances, or earnest skits about the issues of the day. Collaborating with children can also produce edgy – and often funny – boundary-pushing, politically charged work – the kind of work we value in the contemporary performance and visual arts contexts.

The quality of this work is due, in part, to the atypical but strong artistic skills of the children. These skills lie in the realm of spontaneous expression, play, and their ability to pretend, to invent complicated worlds, and to ask challenging and often unanswerable questions. These are all skills that artists need, but only the best manage to acquire. Kelly O'Brien's beautiful film *How Does Life Live?*[10] is a great example. Created in collaboration with her daughters, Emma and Willow, the film is simply a series of questions the two children have posed to O'Brien over the years: *How does life live? Why don't worms have faces? Why don't boys let their hair grow?* As we hear the children ask these beguiling questions, we see them exploring the natural world together: picking flowers, stepping in puddles, climbing hills. Making quality, complex work with child collaborators is a function of simply refraining from making work about sugarplum fairies and, instead, engaging with complicated, challenging ideas. In short, not underestimating the intelligence of the kids.

But beyond a deft incorporation of the participation of children as co-creators, as O'Brien did through her years-long script development with Emma and Willow, collaborating with kids can deploy their presence in even more subversive ways, altering the way we are together, tapping delicately on the social structure, looking to free the diamond of a new social contract. Working with children, then, requires two different understandings of their role. On the one hand, they are like any adult collaborator, bringing to the table ideas and opinions about the work we're creating together. On the other, they are themselves, in effect, artistic material. Their presence, especially the role they play in a relational dynamic with an adult audience, produces outcomes that can be framed nicely as art but that operate at the register of what is really happening: life. This is an understanding of performance that is different than typical forms of representation, where children and adults alike perform fictional characters and situations. And an understanding of performance as modelling possible universes – a universe where children are sovereign, for example.

In the early 2000s, there was much debate in the art world about collaborations that included a high degree of public participation. Leading the discussion was Nicolas Bourriaud, then the director of Paris's Palais de Toyko, whose 1998 book *Relational Aesthetics* brought the question of an activist artistic engagement back into the spotlight, where it now remains, after a couple of decades in the shadows. He maintains that the modernist revolutionary impulse that expected art to usher in a utopian world has not gone anywhere but has shifted now toward modelling possible universes or 'micro-topias' in real time and real places. Rather than radical opposition that promised a major and sudden system-wide rewiring of social relations – a.k.a. a revolution – art was now 'learning to inhabit the world in a better way.'[11]

The art world's response to Bourriaud was strong, if divided, but he provided hope, particularly among artists committed to social justice who had been sidelined and framed as naive since the late 1970s – only suckers think they can change the world, and if you were a revolutionary, you were, at best, an embarrassed one. Debates about ethics and aesthetics between critics, practitioners, and scholars began appearing in the pages of *Artforum*, *October*, and many other of the discipline's leading publications and academic journals. This sharp turn toward the social as artistic material that has occurred over the last twenty years in the visual and performing arts has been assigned various names, each reflecting a slight variation in framing: 'dialogical art,' 'littoral art,' 'new genre public art,' with consensus seeming to coalesce more or less around the term 'social practice.' But, whatever you feel like calling it, what it does is use art as a magical shroud to drape over atypical activities, allowing unusual social configurations or realities to exist, if only for the moment of a performance.

Charting the movement's progress through the 1990s, Bourriaud describes the '[p]ossibility of a relational art – an art taking as its theoretical horizon the realm of human interactions and its social context, rather than the assertion of an independent and private symbolic space … ' Furthermore, this art, so far as Bourriaud can tell, 'points to a radical upheaval of the aesthetic, cultural and political goals introduced by modern art.'[12] He then traces the roots of this upheaval to a global generalization of the urban form and 'extension of this city model to more or less all cultural phenomena.' We're all in this damn thing together, whether we're in Mumbai or Medicine Hat. The use of social relations as material, participatory forms, and art-as-social-research has become a consistent feature of contemporary visual art, performance, and theatre, even finding its way into literary form, and is present in much of the emerging artistic forms fostered by the internet and other communication technologies. Children, with their various abilities, fit nicely into this world, carrying the significance of their childishness, a position of radical otherness in relation to adults, and within this realm there exists great potential to test the idea of ramping up the participation of children.

When considering the social as material for an artistic practice, children, because they are always subject to the dictates of others, offer interesting opportunities to examine aspects of our world that are usually so taken for granted that they are completely hidden. Children are naturally well-suited to these powerful collaborations because of their position within the social structure: they are weak. But that weakness, when deployed artistically as strength, can have reality-bending effects. Their presence alone poses challenges to the very idea of equity, since they are always at risk of being deprived of legal standing. Because of this lack of official status, where they might otherwise possess something with which to leverage power, children force adults into a fascinating corner, where adults are denied all but two options. Adults can negotiate with the children in a non-hierarchical manner, listen to the kids' concerns, and work together in a way that is agreeable to all. Or, conversely, adults can resort to commanding the children, telling them what to do, usually framed in terms of two motivations: expediency and for-their-own-good. These motivations have too long governed the actions of adults in relation to children. The addiction to expediency and for-their-own-good, the little lies we tell kids to make happen the things we're convinced must happen, are defining traits of our society. We deploy them constantly, shamelessly, and often with a shared chuckle among the adults present. It is evidence of our love of speed and of our own interpretation over what is right and respect for multiple viewpoints, our embrace of convenience and ease even as it is often unhealthy or unwanted, our constant drive toward efficiency and the perceived supremacy of our view of the world over that of others: children. Because of the lack of avenues for negotiating with children – we don't allow them to work and make their own income, for example, which would provide things around which to structure a negotiation – those are the two options that children tend to present adults. Children force adults to be either anarchists or authoritarians.

In the world of adult-to-adult interaction, there are shades of grey: negotiations are complex, and getting people to do want you want comes in many sophisticated forms, including immediate or future payments, job promises, fame, or even just a vague idea that whatever you're suffering through will have important positive ramifications for your future. The older we get, the more sophisticated become the ways in which people try to sit us down, shut us up, and get us to focus on our work. With kids, most of these fancy ways to motivate don't work so well. Kids are way too smart for that. Being smart in the way kids often are is not about mere knowledge or analytical accuracy applied to experience, producing generalizable insights. Instead, it is about being smart by virtue of valuing the truth in the moment, by responding honestly and immediately: kids' smarts are at the level of *being*, as disenfranchised as that being might be. They resist being incentivized by an abstract future that simply does not exist, and they insist on being rewarded immediately, the experience of being focused often the reward itself. Think of the times, as a child, when you were lost in play for hours, adopting roles and characters, playing in the sand, and making complex worlds. The ability to focus is not the issue: it is a question of what is worth focusing on. This demand to be rewarded immediately, biological at its core, makes children so powerful that, again, they force you to reveal your true stripes: are you an anarchist or an authoritarian?

If we want the full inclusion of children, all of this will have to be scaled back. Expediency and for-their-own-good are the first and key targets of this army of children I'm imagining: the impossibility of conducting business as usual with children underfoot and the new ways we will develop to interact with them and with each other in their presence. I don't expect to see children suddenly finding the contents of board meetings fascinating – that's an ask too great even for myself – but that, over time, small changes in the organization will occur, adapting whatever aspects can be adapted to include their participation. This will become easier and easier as the economy continues the transition into one in which people slide from project to project, the lines between working, volunteering, supporting, building one's resumé, and contributing to the community becoming increasingly porous, with online activities taking that blur even further. Not unlike Dickens's visions of coal-dust-covered kids, the children toiling in our world today – the kids of the knowledge revolution – are finding their daily efforts generating value for others. But unlike the nineteenth-century coal mines, the return to the world of labour has not yet produced the statistics to prove it is a danger; in fact, some insist that work may not be so bad for the little guys.

Recent studies of children and work in affluent society have demonstrated a much more nuanced situation beyond the view that *child labour = bad*. For children, work can produce a sense of being valuable members of specific communities,[13] provide opportunities for learning, and, for those young people who demonstrate little interest in formal education, work is particularly beneficial.[14] In addition, many working children feel that employment provides them with leverage in negotiations within the home.[15] But labour is labour, whether done by children or grown-ups, and as we make efforts to more comprehensively include kids in the world of work, we will need a new approach to understanding professional environments and standards, with the dry inhumanity of the typical day at the office requiring a welcome overhaul to accommodate the presence of children. Again, expediency will likely be the main target, with everyone forced to slow down and negotiate with each other as real humans with real feelings and desires.

In the chapter 'Children vs. Social Acupuncture,' I will return to the question of working with children in an artistic context to model possible universes, again asserting the idea that arts and culture, particularly performance where people encounter each other in real life, hold especially strong promise for helping us explore the possibilities and benefits of the increased participation of children. But, for now, the next chapter, 'Children vs. Work,' is a deeper look at the world of work because, as much as including children's participation in all matters affecting them has the potential to radically alter our world for the better, the world of work must be understood as a primary spot to roll out the idea of increased participation. Work will allow the kids to participate in creating and exchanging their own value, thereby levelling the playing field and freeing them from their dependence on adults, which will, in turn, allow them to participate in questions of morality and ethics on their own terms, and much more forcefully. This, again, will benefit all, as the virus of a new social contract spreads and influences all matters affecting children, which is, again, to say: everything.

But more than just a simple argument insisting that the kids be put back to work, the next chapter is really about taking a close look at the situation as it stands now and admitting that, in fact, they're *already* doing a lot of unrecognized and unrewarded labour, and we need better systems of accounting to track it, reward it, and grant the kids the influence and power we grant anyone we consider a contributing member of society. Once the little guys are seen as making meaningful, measureable contributions, equal to those of any similar adult, it's then that they will really influence the world, as their wishes are taken into account in areas as straightforward as, for example, urban design. My guess: playgrounds, lots and lots of playgrounds, and playgrounds are not known for their ability to generate a profit. Children: 1, Capitalism: 0.

2

CHILDREN VS. WORK

The exclusion of children from the formal economy deprives them of one of the key leveraging mechanisms available to adults: negotiation. Unemployed adults are also deprived of social standing, have little to bargain with, and are often subject to state control and interference, rendered dependent on others. Just like children. Work – the ability to produce, control, and exchange value – is fundamental to being considered a legitimate person. Children are almost entirely barred from producing any value within the formal economy, and, for the most part, are only understood to be vacuuming up resources through their never-ending needs and demands. Children's relation to the world of work is, in part, a question of their economic worth, which is generally understood to be less than nothing – they're a liability, a burden. If the goal is to increase children's participation in the social machinery, then we're also talking about growing the possibility of their contribution to the world of work, both through increasing their value-producing activities and by acknowledging where they might now already be producing unaccounted-for value.

There is a strong antipathy toward the idea of children working, sometimes shading into prejudice against anyone who might expect or need young people to contribute to the economy, even if we're only talking about the very circumscribed economy of the family. Not that we shouldn't be clear about what constitutes appropriate ways for children to labour. Righteous indignation and concern is absolutely in order when the work is of the worst form, as with the undeniable and clear exploitation of child labour in sweltering factories. That's not what I'm talking about.

Once, in the very early days of *Haircuts by Children*, when the performance was being presented at a theatre festival in the U.K., one of the festival staff, in a moment of typical tension over logistics, snarled angrily that the project was 'child labour.' I'd heard variations of this comment as a joke, but this speaker was serious. Others have also raised concerns about the project: Nicholas Ridout from the University of London called *Haircuts by Children* 'service economy performance,'[16] arguing that instead of engaging in the *representational* labour of playing a character, the kids are actually performing the labour of a hairstylist. He interpreted the labour as real but framed as aesthetic experience because they're kids. He was right. I can easily accept that the kids in *Haircuts by Children* are engaged in service work – it's the whole point of the project – and not a representational performance, and that their labour is real (for which they are compensated). What's actually at issue is the distinction between labour that exploits the child workers and labour that empowers them, which *Haircuts by Children* does. Just ask any of the hundreds of kids who've euphorically appeared in the project and walked home at the end of the day with a bit of cash to spend however they want.

What the UN's agency for dealing with labour standards, the International Labour Organization, defines as unacceptable child labour is 'work that deprives children of their childhood, their potential and their dignity, and that is harmful to physical and mental development.'[17] The ILO is clear that not all work by children is exploitative child labour; it 'depends on the child's age, the type and hours of work performed, the conditions under which it is performed … not all work done by children should be classified as child labour that has to be targeted for elimination.' The ILO lists a number of jobs that young people do that are not a problem: helping out around the house, assisting in the family business, or earning pocket money outside of school hours. They additionally emphasize that the exploitative kind of labour 'interferes with their schooling by: depriving them of the opportunity to attend school; obliging them to leave school prematurely; or requiring them to attempt to combine school attendance with excessively long and heavy work.' In general, the prioritization of schooling is a big piece of the reason why people often have a strong negative reaction to the idea of children in the workforce. While it is true that school does tend to predict for higher incomes later in life,[18] it is not clear if this correlates to the knowledge schooling provides or to the possession of school credentials, which may be valued regardless of the knowledge imparted in the classroom. In which case, school also can qualify as activity that produces and can be considered work, a position held by many sociologists of childhood.

Work, then, given the right conditions and context, is not only okay for children, it can be a valuable piece in their development (just like it can be for adults). So, let's get kids to work, provided that labour happens in a context where they are granted fair treatment, fair compensation, and control of the economic value they generate. In terms of the arts and cultural sector, we're more or less good to go, with Article 8 of the Minimum Age Convention, 1973 (No. 138), stating, 'children may, after consultation with the organizations of employers and workers concerned, be employed for purposes of participation in artistic performances.' The U.K.'s Children and Young Persons Act simply requires a licence for anyone under thirteen to work on film sets and theatre stages.[19] Interestingly, if you're not paying the kids, you don't have to get a licence.

But beyond these straightforward questions of discerning between work that can be understood as child labour and work that is actually okay, there's the trickier question of the work that young people are doing now that is not understood – or not *yet* understood – as work. Feminist economists have examined the labour-intensive activities around the home and in the caring for others – labour that tends to be done primarily by women, is rarely directly compensated for, and is unlikely to be tracked through the various official accounting frameworks. This sort of labour taking place in the domestic sphere remains largely invisible as work. British economist Alison M. S. Watson finds that, in the U.K., over 70 per cent of eleven- to fifteen-year-olds work. Everywhere in the world, children cook, clean, and take care of siblings, the elderly, the disabled, as well as alcoholic and drug-addicted parents; they tidy up around the house, do yardwork and laundry, set and clear the table, deal with the dishwasher, wash clothes, iron, cook, shop, garden, and clean the windows.[20] These are jobs that feminist economists have agreed do produce economic value – by allowing others in the family to spend more time working for money, or activities that support work – like the calories that having a home-cooked meal provide or the clean clothing needed in most work environments. Children often do contribute to the family as well as the general economy, but this sort of analytic focus – examining activities that don't exist in any accounting ledgers – can also be extended to other activities children are engaged in, activities that do not, at first glance, appear to generate value, but in reality, and with more complex approaches to accounting, actually do – value that the kids are, for the most part, not permitted to enjoy, let alone control.

Some of this child labour is difficult to perceive without adopting more complex understandings of the oftentimes-exploitative relational dynamic between adults and children. Sociologist David Oldman gives us a useful way of conceptualizing this dynamic in an odd, original, and often-referenced 1994 article, 'Adult-Child Relations as Class Relations.' Oldman applies a class analysis to the relationship between adults and children and understands adults as a dominant class economically exploiting children. This analysis goes against the view of some feminist economists, like Nancy Folbre, in her 2008 book *Valuing Children: Rethinking the Economics of the Family*, who details the cost borne by parents as they shoulder the bulk of producing the next generation to their own economic detriment. Oldman avoids thinking of the family as a site of ideological conflict where children are typically framed as either resource-sucking dependents or the targets of abuse and neglect, and instead focuses on understanding how the activities of children produce value for adults.

Adults and children are both involved in a process wherein the adults control and supervise a system of activities that, for the child, constitutes 'growing up.' The activities of children create entire, complex, and constantly churning industries of what Oldman calls 'childwork.' This, he says, refers to the work of adults, not children, and he chooses the term 'because of its theoretical closeness to "housework" and even "shitwork," the evocative term used by some feminist writers to describe the low-status labour involved in the care and maintenance of others.'[21]

In childwork, the child is the object of the labour of others. At the same time, however, the child is an active subject. It is the child's activity, the child's own labour, that becomes the object of adult labour, providing the means of subsistence for a significant proportion of the adult population. This can range from the natural activities of the child that need supervision at the daycare, a good deal of non-instructional time at school, as well as the many supervised activities that occur extracurricularly or during summer vacation: camp, sports, and artistic activities. Oldman claims '"growing up" is constituted as a pattern of activities that define, and are defined by, many of the private profit-making service industries, and provide many jobs in the public sector.'[22]

Further, this is an *exploitative* relationship – Oldman shows that the value of childwork to adults grows at the expense of the value to children, which he calls 'a "generational" mode of production.' He notes the lack of a connection between the growth or shrinking in service provision for children and their actual needs, pointing out that this growth or shrinking is based on political squabbles over the likes of taxes and transfer payments. It's got nothing to do with what the kids need.

Oldman looks at two examples where he sees an exploitative relationship between children and adults: schooling and childcare.

For the most part, school attendance is compulsory and non-negotiable, and children have little say in the quality of the time spent in the classroom. Oldman observes that teachers' salaries, not direct services to the children, take the lion's share of the resources, with very high student-to-teacher ratios creating an unfavourable situation for the children. Nonetheless, most people clearly differentiate school from work, a practice many sociologists of childhood disagree with. Danish sociologist Jens Qvortrup is particularly adamant about this point,[23] coming at the question from a different angle than Oldman. Qvortrup's argument is that over the course of different historical eras, children have always contributed in some way. During the agrarian era, they pitched in on the farm along with everyone else; during the early days of the industrial era, they worked in factories; and, since the turn of last century, those children living in affluent societies are 'employed' doing schoolwork. He points out that while, in the first two instances, it was generally the parents who captured the value, with the transition to modernity and compulsory schooling, it's the state that benefits, with the production of a future labour force. Schooling, he says, contributes to the forming of human capital, but this is strictly credited to the teachers, who are understood to be filling the children with knowledge; however, as he writes, 'how does one imagine it to be received, embodied, carried through the medium and made active without the help of the child's own capacities and competencies?' He goes on: 'if children are themselves adding to human capital formation in contributing to the enhancement of knowledge – should we not then be inclined to also include them into our systems of reward and distribution?'[24]

In the case of childcare as childwork, Oldman notes the rise of the participation of women in the labour market and the corresponding rise of childcare that now takes place outside of the family. Childcare occurring in the family is uncompensated and unaccounted for, but, as it has been commercialized, Oldman argues that it is an instance of the raw material of children's activities needing the control, and refinement, of paid adults, even if the pay is hardly opulent. In both cases, school and childcare, the claim Oldman makes is fairly straightforward: the quality of life of adults is increased by their control over the process of the growing up of children, while the quality of life for children is reduced.

Peter Gray, American developmental psychologist, founder and director of the National Institute for Play, and author of *Free to Learn*, describes schooling as '*imprisonment*.' He points out that, since 1955, as children's time spent in free play – play without adult supervision – has plummeted, there been a commensurate rise in psychopathology in children and adolescents: anxiety, depression, helplessness, and narcissism are rampant.[25] While he admits it's difficult to establish causation, he cites the many studies that have shown the benefits of play in both humans and animals. One benefit is particularly relevant:

the fact that play contributes to young people developing a sense of control over their environment, their bodies, their emotions, their goals, and their relationships with others. As free play has declined, so too has the feeling that young people have that they are well prepared to deal with the world. Without the physical, emotional, and social risks that young people take as they play with each other, risks that simply cannot occur under the constant supervision of adults, they fail to develop the resilience required to feel confident and in control. The risks involved in exploring the nooks, crannies, and far reaches of their neighbourhood, getting lost on the streets of their city, or splashing through streams and climbing trees in natural surroundings provide children with the fortitude to navigate life without succumbing to paralyzing fear and depression. But while children pay for this lack of playtime with their health, adults actually make money from it, as they are compensated for running the various activities that now occupy children's time, or profit directly, generating revenue from many of the digital and screen-based activities that have also replaced free play.

This lack of access to free play has a related phenomenon that stretches into the world of adults, with the evolving and changing face of the world of work in the twenty-first century infiltrating adults' leisure time as well. So many of our activities – work and play – either do actually produce value, or occur trapped within areas where value is being exchanged or produced. Nicolas Bourri-aud, in *Relational Aesthetics*, observes that 'before long, it will not be possible to maintain relationships between people outside [these] trading areas. So here we are summonsed to talk about things around a duly priced drink, as a symbolic form of contemporary human relations.' It's difficult to form meaningful relations without the presence of commercial activities, and children are very much partici-pating in this trend.

In addition to the creep of commerce into every fissure of our lives, there is also the very real shift in the way the face of work presents itself and the evolving activities that are now – more and more – to be understood as, in fact, work. This change in how we work is rapidly reintegrating children in ways that are yet to be fully understood. In fact, children are well positioned to not only benefit from these changes but also to lead some of the innovations, whose stirrings can be observed in the central role that young people play on the internet, particularly through social media. German education scholar Dieter Kirchhofer points to the fragmentation of labour markets, the expansion of work from nine-to-five at a desk to the entire day, with the possibility of almost constant work. This fragmentation, he claims, 'will also change the children's relationship to the adult world of work, and ... new possibilities will open up for children to integrate into that world.'[26]

Work's infiltration into all aspects of life results in the ubiquity of what French sociologists Luc Boltanski and Ève Chiapello call the 'projective city,' where networks of interlocking projects characterize vast areas of the world of work, which they contrast to two periods in the past: the 'commercial city' (1930–60s), where a lifelong commitment to the company was the hallmark of the 'great man' (think of the retiring employees of yesteryear who gave their entire careers to one organization and their golden pocket-watch moment) and, further back, the 'industrial city,' where the 'great men' were more likely to be captains of industry, with a focus on entrepreneurialism (American industrialist Andrew Carnegie, for example). They claim that, these days, *project* organization has become the way in which society at large is conceived and organized, and people's greatness is measured by *activity*, with success often calculated in terms of busyness.

This sense of busyness, and therefore of demonstrable success, is not dependent on a person's income or ability to produce; '[a]ctivity in the projective city surmounts the oppositions between work and non-work, the stable and the unstable, wage-earning class and non-wage-earning class, paid work and voluntary work, that which may be assessed in terms of productivity and that which, not being measurable, eludes calculable assessment.'[27] Claiming you're super-busy, the new hallmark of the 'great man,' is synonymous with claiming to be super-successful. Until recently, it was easy to distinguish when a person was working and when they were not working.

When you were working, you were unambiguously earning a paycheque. Things are no longer that clear, with the proliferation of unpaid internships and other volunteer labour being a requirement for getting a foothold and surviving in many industries – particularly the arts and culture sector. Even unpaid attendance at a whole range of events – like launches, openings, performances, symposia, conferences, talks – must be understood as a necessary activity for success and, therefore, is clearly a form of labour. Unlike waged work, this new type of activity easily incorporates children, where activities like volunteering are not just things young people do for pleasure or leisure, to build a resumé or prepare for their eventual economic participation – these activities *are* economic participation.

This sort of analysis still approaches the question of children's labour through the typical frame, with labour understood as producing a value that a measure such as the GDP can assess. The kids, like the rest of us, volunteer and attend those launches, openings, performances, symposia, and talks for their intrinsic worth, which includes the value to our careers, which eventually produces – or so we hope – value that can be translated into more power or influence, or deposited into a bank. These are still typical accounting measures, but other measures exist, like the idea of well-being.

Measuring a population's well-being is gaining traction as a better means of assessing the health of a society than measuring the production of outputs, which tends to be riddled with perverse incentives: inefficient spending by a government is accounted for no differently than spending that is carefully and rationally targeted. France's Commission on the Measurement of Economic Performance and Social Progress, led by economist Joseph Stiglitz, asserts that profit should be defined multidimensionally, with leisure needing to be assigned a value. This is another area where the contribution of children can be reassessed and given worth. The play and playfulness children bring to the table can be seen as another contribution of value they make to the lives of adults, though in this case, the relationship is not exploitative. Again, children's natural impulses and activities provide value by reminding us that one of the essential parts of a holistic life is fun. As an example, I was sitting in a café trying to get some work done and noticed a family at an adjacent table: a child aged maybe one, a mother and father, and a grandfather. The grandfather was, by any normal standards of adult behaviour, acting like an idiot: babbling, gurgling, issuing elongated vowels, his eyes wide and unblinking. Was he having a stroke? No. He was just talking to the baby.

He was playing with sounds, gestures, facial expressions, and he probably thought he was doing it strictly for the benefit of the little kid. But according to Stuart Brown, the author of *Play: How It Shapes the Brain, Opens the Imagination, and Invigorates the Soul* and the director of the National Institute for Play, there's a massive body of evidence from across the whole scientific spectrum that play is an important biological process that not only contributes to our development when we are growing up, but continues to do so into adulthood, helping us to continue to survive, by sustaining complex social groups as well as contributing to innovation and creativity.[28] The important effects of play do not change as we age; what does change, according to Kathryn Hirsh-Pasek, director of the Temple University Infant & Child Laboratory, is the stigma associated with play: 'We associate play with childhood, and therefore "playing" with childishness.'

That's where kids come in.[29] Children give permission for adults to play without accruing stigma. This adds real value to an adult's life, a value that escapes the typical accounting in measures like the GDP, but can be accounted for when we take our eyes off monetary measures and focus on well-being. Those contributing to, or even forcing, leisure (i.e., children) must have their contribution given some sort of economic valuation or understanding. Taking Stiglitz's logic further, the play that children allow adults to enjoy can also be understood as being economically valuable.

Another area where we may be underestimating the economic and social contributions of children lies in a quirk of sociology. When a person – particularly a man – becomes a parent, after a certain age, they may well find their social value increases. Children can sometimes legitimize adults in the eyes of other adults. This can be seen acutely in the lives of male politicians who haul their families into the spotlight, splashing them all over their websites. The first sentence of Canada's superstar prime minister's bio on his website describes Justin Trudeau as 'a teacher, father, advocate and leader.' In the U.K.'s recent Labour leadership race, Owen Smith contrasted himself with one of his opponents, the gay and childless Angela Eagle: 'I'm normal,' he said. 'I've got a wife and three children.' Within a strictly political calculation, parenthood, then, is often linked to normalcy and efficacy as a leader. While, for women in the workforce, parenthood is often a liability, within wider considerations, children tend to legitimize both women and men. The web is teeming with articles written by both women and men fighting back against the stigma of childlessness, strongly asserting their life is meaningful despite the fact they have no kids, which implies pretty big social forces suggesting otherwise.

This value-added is obviously not at the expense of the children, so the relationship cannot be described as exploitative, but it does remain true that the presence of children alone can be enough to produce positive economic effects that are captured by the children's parents, even as, at other times – single motherhood, for example – children are a liability.

But the power of parenthood, the play that children bring and the reframing of much of their participation in the world as work, are instances where I resort to a deconstruction and a re-seeing of circumstances where the activities in question are very much hidden from the sites that produce the sort of value that is easy to measure: money. But the kids also labour in activities that are very, very close to the site where monetary value is being generated.

The sun was shining brightly as I arrived at Toronto's Distillery District for the presentation of *Kids' Table*, my project involving over a hundred children working in collaboration with twenty-five local chefs. I had put some serious thought into what I was wearing: a brown polka-dotted shirt, green pants, and bright blue shoes. I just needed a bow tie. With only an hour until the launch, the chances of finding one were slim, but dropping into a shop, I found a beautiful striped green bow tie that, playfully clashing with my polka dots, completed the picture. I told the shop owner I'd only buy it on the condition that she would tie it for me – I needed it sorted *now*. She said her husband usually tied them, but it was time she learned. She loaded up a YouTube video and we got to work. After a few complicated, hard-to-follow tutorials failed us, she eventually found a winner: *How to Tie a Bow Tie for Dummies*,[30] by Benjamin Kipps, who looked about twelve. Ben's innovation, elevating his video above all others, was that he used software to reverse it, providing a mirror image of himself – not even the experts at bowtie.com had managed to make it this simple. This was not just kid-smart, but smart-smart. In the comments on Ben's video, dozens of people express gratitude, respect for his innovation, and surprise that, after they'd struggled with many other videos, this one by a little kid solved it for them. And, of course, for me. I stepped out of the shop and into the radiant sunshine and my colleagues' compliments.

Ben's video is a great example of all the unpaid work happening on the internet, often produced by young people, and often almost directly producing monetary value. While helping someone tie a bowtie might seem like plain old neighbourly behaviour, it becomes something quite different when the tutorial is for a specific piece of software, for example, where the developers are provided an army's worth of free IT help by these young people. Whether this labour is exploitation or not (I don't think it is) is irrelevant; the fact remains that it *is* labour – labour that is generating monetary value. If I can't easily use a piece of software, I probably won't continue to use it or promote it to my colleagues. Young people are central to this and other industries. The makeup industry, for example, benefits from the bazillions of tutorial videos out there of young girls and boys, some as young as four, breaking down exactly how to produce a particular look with a particular product. One standout is the U.K.'s Kian Paul Owen, known as SimplyKian!, who started creating makeup tutorials on YouTube at age ten and now has almost 100,000 people following his detailed and thorough instructions, complete with mention of the brand of every single product he uses. Surprising – and further evidence that the kids have got their shit together – is Kian's vocal dedication to LGBT rights, in particular the op-ed videos he makes with his boyfriend, where they demonstrate Kian's motto: 'Being true to who you are is the most beautiful thing you can be.'

'Teens, Social Media and Technology Overview 2015,' an American Pew Foundation study, found that 24 per cent of American teens go online 'almost constantly,' with 92 per cent online daily. Despite reports of its uncoolness, in 2015 Facebook remained the most popular forum, with Instagram and Snapchat following. None of this would surprise anyone who works with young people. Nor is it surprising that when the Pew Foundation says 'constantly,' they really do mean constantly. In an informal survey of over thirty of the teens I work with (conducted through Facebook, of course), I learned that almost all of them sleep with their smartphones, as do many of us.

Back in the days before the internet, the people who generated the content that drew our eyes and ears to ads were often paid well for that service: the rock stars on the radio, popular DJs and radio hosts, all the people producing television shows: actors, writers, directors, producers, etc. These days the users of these digital platforms, many of them young people, produce a whole chunk of that content and produce it for nothing. Facebook would not exist without the armies of kids (and the rest of us) producing piles and piles of content to pull in each other's eyes to gaze at the ads and click on the 'Like' button, donating valuable data. Children and young people are participating in this as much as the rest of us – they are, in fact, often at the centre of it, driving the whole operation. The latest hot thing in social media always first takes hold among the kids. Young people, whose voracious and constant use drives the sector's innovation, populate many apps, like Snapchat, which is not only used extensively and overwhelmingly by young people, but was invented by a small crew of three twenty-one-year-olds, who are now zillionaires.

For more evidence of the monetary value children are bringing to the tech world, we can look to video games. The sector is one of the biggest in the world,[31] with the Chinese market worth US$24 billion, the American market worth US$23 billion, and the U.K. market US$5 billion.[32] While the activities of the young people are not drawing eyes to ads or producing personal data to be sold, the relationship between the adults who make the games and the young people who play them could be described as exploitative. The adults have figured out how to take the raw materials of childhood – the desire and need to play – and divert these activities off the streets and parks, where they produced little value for adults, to package them in addictive and expensive experiences. Children's natural and spontaneous activities are steered away from a kind of play that is devised and controlled by children – where the 'means of production' are 'owned' by the children as they run around outside, using whatever natural 'toys' they find among the sticks and rocks of the world. Instead, these impulses are deftly brought into the world of the economic, where adults own these means of play and the children's activities are harnessed, refined, and shaped for a whole ton of adult profit.

This chapter has looked at the activities of children that are really work that directly produces monetary value, as well as those that escape the typical accounting frameworks, hoping to illuminate areas where we can agree that young people are actually producing value. How to acknowledge and reward this participation is another question altogether, but one we need to answer for more than just children. Many of the value-producing activities I mention above are activities that adults also engage in, while also being paid nothing. This, again, is primarily due to the shifting face of work in the twenty-first century, where it has deftly leapt beyond the nine-to-five and, particularly for many of us in arts and culture, managed to spill into our entire lives, sweeping along our children, who participate side by side with the best of us adults. One possible option to address this is the idea of the 'universal guaranteed income' or 'basic income,' where everyone, including young people, would receive an income transfer sufficient to meet their basic needs, generated through publicly owned means or taxation. This idea has gained traction on both the left and right, for a variety of ideological and practical reasons, and is being tested in the U.S., Finland, Holland, and Canada, among other countries. Understanding the economic contribution of children in the way I have outlined strongly supports the idea that even young children should be divvied up a slice of the basic income pie – fair is fair.

But, in contrast to the reframing and deconstruction necessary to understand the value that children are already contributing and whatever redistributive methods are deployed to redress it, a more direct way of increasing the agency of young people in the world is to simply put them to work – for real – in what we all understand work to be: labour brought to the market and exchanged directly for monetary value. While more straightforward than identifying all the different areas of hidden value production that kids are now doing, putting kids to work is actually much more difficult to imagine implementing. Children employed in the workplace? Am I off my head? But maybe the inclusion of kids, here too, can be of more-than-monetary benefit and, ultimately, contribute to an increase in well-being for everyone.

Working with children in terms of *being* rather than *becoming* means we have to abandon some cherished notions of professional and workplace conduct. While 'professionalism' usually means having certain technical skills, Jeff Schmidt in *Disciplined Minds* asserts that professionals work within 'an assigned political and ideological framework,' where those 'who stubbornly continue to value human contact are handicapped.' Schmidt observes that 'work in general is becoming more and more ideological, and so is the workforce that does it,' with those 'whose "bad attitude" would undermine work-place discipline' being scrutinized and squeezed out.[33]

Children, most of whom have not internalized the discipline to stifle boredom or repress feelings, and who tend to act without concern for the smooth sailing of unimpeded and unfeeling produc-tivity, were squeezed out of the professional sphere over a century ago and are either stuck at school – another venue where feelings are not welcome – or are cloistered in one of the only institutions left where complex and messy feelings are permitted: the family. The workplace is a site where things like boredom and temper tantrums are not cool. This is the case, even as we all, at times, suffer acute boredom with our work and are forced to keep a tight lid on anything resembling a meltdown. The workplace is a realm of deep dishonesty, as we must keep it together or at least fake it, even as the inbox – and our brains – threatens to explode. The weight of this dishonesty is borne by children, the childlike, and those who don't feel like lying. People have feelings. It's okay.

The process of professionalization begins in earnest, at a very young age, in our first encounter with the school system, where language and actions are strictly policed, and young people are inculcated into a deeply ideological framework that includes surrendering one's will and following instructions, whether or not those instructions make any sense. School forces young people to adhere to a rigid schedule, regardless of personal rhythms and desires. And it's in the classroom where we produce probably the modern worker's strongest skill: tolerance of boredom. We learn to live in the anaesthetic mode.

A firewall has been erected between the making of money and the living of life, not because life stops when people enter their workplace – of course it doesn't – but because the living of life tends to get in the way of the making of money. It is much easier to make money when you stop worrying about pesky things like feelings. Attempts to impose an order on the mess it is to be human, an order that cruelly excises feelings, are always doomed to fail. This failure, however, comes at the expense of compassion and civility, when normal feelings are subject to inhuman and Kafkaesque disciplinary actions.

Children and the childlike – those of us who are not so good at or not so interested in stifling normal feeling that gets in the way of productivity, those who can't find our footing in an atmosphere of an austere professionalism that deftly conceals itself through the crypto-fascism of 'best practices' – are the target of any number of adultitarian manoeuvres: shushing of all stripes, our actions constantly subjected to the scrutiny of those who demand that the workplace is no place for honesty or life.

This view is blared through the conservative rallying cry 'life-work balance!' If work is not life, then what exactly is it? Death?

When children are added to any environment, death goes out the window, but at the necessary cost of adding feelings – those awkward, ugly, hopeful things. Accepting feelings is to accept that discomfort is okay and to understand that any workplace without feelings is a workplace in the service of a deeply conservative, factory-like mentality where emotions, which distinguish us from ants, are banned. Children rebel against this and there's nothing ideological about it. It is ontological: it is who they are, and we need them to lead the way, as murky as this way might be. But that's part of the challenge of this proposal: I don't know where it will end up, I just know that when a child loves or hates someone, they simply state it. This clarity and honesty breaks through the hypocrisy of professionalism, bringing humanity back into the boardroom.

3

CHILDREN VS. SOCIAL ACUPUNCTURE

The proposal in this book is a form of what I playfully call social acupuncture: the needling and poking of social dynamics to redirect flows of resources, whether that's cash or ephemeral resources like attention or the right to have one's concerns taken seriously.[34] Social acupuncture is driven by an aesthetic of civic engagement, an understanding of beauty that recognizes the relatively newly minted power of art and culture to meaningfully intervene in the social sphere. It is the use of social relations as material in an artistic practice, toward both social and aesthetic ends. The word *aesthetic* here is used in its original sense as being the opposite of a numbing of feeling[35] — anesthetic. An aesthetic of civic engagement is feeling-filled engagement with the various institutions of civil society. It is the idea of our lives as a form of social performance, where beauty is found in small places like harmony, friendship, or the challenging awkwardness of simply getting to know someone.

As I mentioned, I'm an embarrassed revolutionary, stoked and ready to fight the evil powers of oppression but mortified by the state of disarray and rabid infighting that my comrades in the activist scene have been forever stuck in. People often reserve their truly scalding critiques for others who are, when considering the long game, their allies. It is much easier to shame someone nearby whose analysis has been diagnosed as 'problematic' than to take on the really nasty people, particularly since the really nasty people are very tough to access. While I am in agreement with the overall objectives of the activist left – fairness, equity, and pushing back against a whole bunch of intersecting oppressions – it worries me, as these days it often seems more interested in identifying monsters to vilify than actually producing improvements.

My intention with the social acupuncture work is to sidestep this problem altogether, but rather than working in opposition, challenging those things I want eradicated, I prefer to work propositionally: proposing, devising, and demonstrating alternative ways of being together that obliquely oppose the horrors of the world by simply doing something different. This isn't like those artists who avoid activism, confident their focus on individual change and creative expression is enough, with hipsters like Patti Smith eschewing political movements and soaking up the decay of New York like she was watching a film in the air-conditioned comfort of a cinema.[36] I'm not referring to individualism at all, or even creative expression, for that matter – I'm talking about exploring the aesthetic power of *relationships*, and forming new relationships necessarily involves some awkwardness and discomfort. Requiring children to conquer shyness and interact with adults in many of my performances – like *Haircuts by Children* – has often been credited with sustained changes in the young people, who are exhilarated to discover themselves treated as equals.

Social evolution, growth, and change crawl slowly along upon the back of discomfort. Building bridges across social divides and shifting social dynamics so that resources flow in new directions means inserting ideas and taking actions that, at times, can be uncomfortable. An analogy with physical and intellectual growth is helpful: it's impossible to build physical strength without pushing muscles to the point of discomfort, and it's impossible to build intellectual strength without the discomfort of conceptual confusion. In the first case, we've got 'no pain, no gain,' and in the second, 'no confusion, no clarity.' With social growth, we can say 'no awks, no alliances' (*awks* being an awkward situation). Without direct human interaction between opposing populations, only the short-term and the less-than-ideal solution of *tolerance* is possible. Tolerance is hardly a principle upon which to build a movement capable of confronting the scale of contemporary inequity. What we need is friendship and empathy.

In my experience, friendship and empathy tend to develop naturally when people are placed in close proximity and work together toward a shared goal. Neo-Nazis and other hardcore racists have been shown to revise their hateful position through straightforward, casual contact with those they vilify. Those they hate turn out to be people just like them. The answer isn't to push away people whose views we disagree with – no matter how hate-filled or repugnant their beliefs – but, where possible, to bring those people even closer, where the effects of one another's simple, straightforward humanity can erode the more recalcitrant and nasty views. This is not easy to do, and there's a risk of continuing to traumatize the traumatized, which must be avoided. But building walls or calling for muscle to deal with the situation violently – like former University of Missouri communications professor Melissa Click, who was caught on camera calling for 'muscle' to remove journalists during anti-racism protests – is probably is not the best answer.

To bring people together in this way, there needs to be a stealth element to social acupuncture: diversions and decoys to distract people from fear and hatred with simple acts of artistic irreverence and playfulness. I try to devise other possible worlds, even if they are roped off within the relatively non-threatening corral of an art project: these are the microtopias of Bourriaud.

The notion of artists using art as a tool to create social change has made some confident strides over the last couple of decades: there's been a proliferation of discussions of art and activism, with the mushrooming of university courses and even full programs focused on this question. But I'm looking for an atomic accelerator to smash people together at high speeds, hoping to bypass knee-jerk resistance to change and get people to encounter each other with more openness. The discomfort arising from social acupuncture is my accelerator, and the strange, irreverent activities are the speed that knocks people off their feet and into a state where their irrational prejudices melt away.

While this might sound hopelessly naive, insights from the worlds of analytic sociology and the science of dynamics provide a way for us to start thinking about how small artistic social interventions can lead to larger, system-wide change.

Since introducing the idea of an aesthetic of civic engagement in *Social Acupuncture*, I've expanded the thinking to include the idea of social relations as a primary material for an artistic practice. This shift in focus from the institutions of civil society to simply the interactions between individuals is supported with insights from the fields of analytic sociology and the methodological orientation of what's called 'structural individualism.'

Analytic sociology tries to explain a social phenomenon by detailing the mechanisms that bring about that phenomenon. These mechanisms are always considered in terms of the actions of individuals and the relations between them. It doesn't matter how macro the social phenomenon, be it neighbourhood segregation, low scholastic achievement of certain demographics, different mortality rates for people with different income levels, and on and on. All of these phenomena come into being through interactions between *individuals.*

Systemic racism and sexism, for example, are mostly realized in interactions between small groups of people, often between two individuals: a landlord rejecting an applicant, a cop shooting a Black man, a boss promoting an inexperienced man over an experienced woman. The convenient shorthand typically used is that 'society' is responsible for this 'systemic bias,' and, while that language is often true enough to facilitate a more or less coherent conversation, it is often not up to the task of solving the problem. What is 'society,' after all, but a bunch of people interacting with each other in very small configurations? Social facts must be explained in terms of the intended and unintended results of the actions of *individuals*, while still taking into account the effects of the various social and institutional structures, dynamics, and positions in which people find themselves. So the focus is on the action of individuals, while still keeping an eye on the social structures and relations that temper, constrain, promote, or otherwise affect these actions.

The risk of focusing on the interactions between individuals is that it reduces life to a series of atomized encounters, allowing people to assume, for example, that one person's chances of success are more or less a matter of working as hard as another person, without considering the different structures in which individuals are fixed. This is the sin of another strain of thinking, 'methodological individualism,' which asserts that people are rational actors always seeking to maximize their advantage, without taking into consideration that the information that any single individual has is never perfect, and that people enter life with different sets of advantages, disadvantages, awarenesses, and blind spots. A Black teen must play Pokémon GO with a different awareness of her or his surroundings than a white teen, as the risks for her are very different and can include being labelled a suspicious person or even held at gunpoint by the police, as in the case of Faith Joseph Ekakitie.[37] But while systemic biases may have set the stage for it, it was not 'the system' that held him at gunpoint, but, rather, a few individual cops. What this means for artistic social practice or, indeed, any intervention, is that the place to begin is between individuals.

The idea that what occurs at the individual level can produce macro-level phenomena is a key insight of the science of complex systems. The science of complexity looks for context-independent dynamics that can be used to understand a wide variety of phenomena, both natural and social. For example, another useful insight from this field is the phase shift or tipping point. In a phase shift, a system goes through a clearly defined transformation and enters a qualitatively different state. Phase shifts can occur in any dynamic system, and when the time is ripe, it takes little to make one happen. For example, water: between one and ninety-nine degrees Celsius, the addition or subtraction of a degree here or there has little effect, but if the water is at either end of that range, a single degree can make all the difference, triggering a drastic phase shift from one state to another, and it becomes either ice or steam. Within social dynamics, phase shifts occur when particular sets of macro social relations suddenly change after a sufficient accumulation of micro, individual-level changes: enough people come to the conclusion that gay marriage is not going to collapse civilization and the idea is passed into law, for example.

For an embarrassed revolutionary reluctant to actually utter the word *revolution*, phase shifts offer an alternative model. And with the departure of the idea of revolution per se, we also say goodbye to the revolutionary vanguard, those who plan and attempt to shape and control social relations according to ideology. Instead, we replace this with the idea of an accumulation of small changes between people whose individual attitudes change, little by little, finally reaching a tipping point when society arrives at a different consensus and ideas are concretized into law or widely held beliefs. Phase shifts, then, provide a model for the role of the artist as relatively relaxed social interventionist, adding a degree here or there, waiting until an aggregation of the micro-level effects of many social actors produce macro-level change.

Through the remainder of the book, I present a case study from my own work to demonstrate the ideas I'm outlining. Since 2005, Mammalian Diving Reflex has been working with a group of young people in Toronto's Parkdale neighbourhood in what was intended to be a one-off project but quickly became an artistic intervention in the lives of a community of people, including myself, my collaborators, my company, my friends, and the cultural sector in general – as well as the lives of the young people, the majority of whom were about nine when we started. As of this writing in early 2017, most are turning twenty-one, two serve on the company's board, one works with us as an accounting assistant and producer in training, one has been hired by one of Canada's most important performing arts festivals as an emerging producer, and about ten regularly travel with us to co-direct our work internationally. We create and present work in Toronto in collaboration with a surrounding community of many youth – and some adults – who check out what we're doing and participate. Mammalian is ramping up this participation over the next few years, passing as many responsibilities to the youth as interest them, in what amounts to a succession plan: giving the kids the key to the company.

The intervention was inspired by *Haircuts by Children* – it was both an artistic and a critical success, but also, most importantly, the performances made a difference in the life of the company and the wider world, if only by spreading the idea that collaborations with children for an adult audience are artistically viable. The impact on the youth – the area of primary interest for most people and certainly most funders – is more difficult to evaluate. I have plenty of testimonials to how much they've learned, how much fun we've had, and how their horizons have been expanded. However, the crucial counterfactual – what would the lives of the youth have looked like had we not all worked together? – is difficult to estimate. One of the youth swears he was on a path to no good before he met us, but he's a brilliant guy and I'm sure he would have been fine.

Nevertheless, because it is an interesting question for the youth arts sector in general, we should note that it has been answered affirmatively: yes, arts engagement does make a statistically significant difference to things like participation, arts skills development, task completion, and pro-social skills,[38] as well as having positive effects on school grades and relationships with parents.[39] For those of us working in the sector, there is nothing surprising about these findings. It is obvious that engaging with art improves young people's lives across many dimensions.

However, each person is a particular case, and the effects of any collaboration need to be evaluated on its own terms. In the chapter entitled 'Children vs. Mammalian Diving Reflex,' I introduce an evaluative framework, designed specifically for the methods I'm proposing here, that places the focus of evaluation as much, if not more, on the organization doing the engaging of the youth than on the youth themselves. If certain things are happening within the organization – things that are much easier to measure than impact on the youth – we can be confident that effects are being felt among the youth. But more on this framework later.

Artistic programs, like any social interventions, can be studied through a realist[40] lens that asks a basic set of questions: what sort of intervention 'works for whom, in what circumstances, in what respects, over which duration ... and why.'[41]

So, to begin this examination of Mammalian's work in Parkdale, I want to take a look at the program theory we used to approach this work: why we chose to do what we did in the place we did it with the people we did it with. Again, within a realist paradigm, we're trying to understand the context (who, where), the mechanisms deployed (what), and the outcomes desired, predicted, or achieved (why). Starting, then, with who and where takes us to Parkdale and the people who share this neighbourhood.

Described in the most simple way, the work in Parkdale was designed to quickly foster creative connections between two populations who share the neighbourhood: artists, who are predominantly white and tend to come from other parts of country (artists from across Canada are drawn to Toronto, Vancouver, and Montreal because of other artists, activities, more generous public funding, and connections to international networks); and the children and young people who have grown up in the neighbourhood, mostly the kids of immigrants and refugees who came to Canada in the late 1970s and 1980s as a result of the immigration policies of Pierre Trudeau.

In Toronto's 2010 statistics, visible minorities accounted for 74 per cent of Parkdale's youth population, with many refugees from places like Vietnam, Sri Lanka, and Tibet. Also, because of historically low rents, Parkdale has a high concentration of artists – in 2010. three of the postal codes in the region clocked in among the ten most highly concentrated areas of artists in the Canada.[42] But this is changing quickly, as both artists and immigrants are being squeezed out by gentrification.

Gentrification is often fuelled by deindustrialization and the concentration of professionals and cultural markets in the core of the city,[43] with a focus on recreation, consumption, production, and pleasure.[44] Artists are sometimes called the 'shock troops of gentrification,' blamed for triggering the changes in a neighbourhood by establishing its viability as a desirable place. However, the presence of artists is neither a sufficient nor necessary precondition for gentrification: neighbourhoods without artists often gentrify, and those with artists sometimes never do. As much as those of us in the sector would love to believe that a bunch of broke-ass hipsters could trigger such a large change, the fact is that nothing happens in neighbourhoods without the city's regulatory permission and the vast amounts of cash that developers bring, attracted much more by a neighbourhood's evolving proximity to expanding business districts or changes to transportation infrastructure. For example, another Toronto neighbourhood in the midst of gentrification is Weston–

Mount Dennis; not particularly known for its concentration of artists, it lies at the centre of a number of public transportation infrastructure initiatives.

Both immigrant families and low-income artists live in Parkdale because of the cheaper rent and proximity to the core of the city and are both subject to what Katie Mazer and Katharine Rankin of the University of Toronto refer to as 'displacement pressure': 'the everyday ways in which people are dislocated from the social spaces of the neighbourhoods.'[45] Mazer and Rankin point out that both real neighbourhood amenities – parks, small businesses, schools, and community centres and the symbolic value attached to these – make Parkdale what it is, and as these shift, they include some people while excluding others, resulting in the dislocation and eventual relocation of people who have considered the neighbourhood home for years. They refer to Tim Butler and Garry Robson's concept of 'tectonic' social relations, in which 'social groups or "plates" overlap or run parallel to one another without much in the way of integrated experience in the areas' social and cultural institutions.'[46]

The changes in Parkdale, particularly along the quickly hip-ifying Queen Street (long synonymous with hipsters, artists, and nightlife) – the equivalent of the high streets of the U.K. – provided an unusual window of opportunity, a short period of time for meaningful connections to be made between these two populations, as they found themselves displaced in the same way and facing similar pressures, in order to address the effects of tectonic social relations. As both populations were/are being squeezed out of the neighbourhood, the work that Mammalian engaged in was to foster an alliance to create connections designed to short-circuit the city's social barriers and address one of the cultural sector's most pernicious shortcomings: cultural uniformity or homogeneity.

Those involved in arts and culture remain predominantly and frustratingly white, a phenomenon that is seen in Canada,[47] the U.K.,[48] the U.S.,[49] Europe, and Australia.[50] But Mammalian's engagement is not at all based on a warm and fuzzy altruistic effort toward a superficial but still-siloed diversity, a point I make in *Social Acupuncture* by citing political philosopher Michael Hardt's call for the unification of charity and desire. For really effective change, acts that benefit others should also benefit oneself. I thought then and know now that these collaborations with the children of Parkdale can produce interesting artistic work as well as social outcomes that bring positive impact to all involved, including my company and myself.

It was with these intentions that I proposed to Parkdale Public School that Mammalian be the artists in residence. Over a number of years we created a series of activities, under the umbrella title Parkdale Primary School vs. Queen Street West (the hip and popular high street in Parkdale), that brought together the children in the school with the artists and other cultural types who shared their streets. The thinking was that – inspired by my experience with *Haircuts by Children* – collaborating on art projects would be an excellent and effective way to create lasting and meaningful friendships that might, over time, develop into full-blown professional relationships and, ultimately, a community. Using Parkdale as an accelerator, I wanted to collide artists and children, like atomic particles, to see if we could release hidden energy, create new social forms, manufacture new ways of being together, and begin to change the face of the cultural sector.

The projects in this chapter are early examples of Mammalian's work with children and, as such, do not offer the most solid evidence for my proposal of ramping up the participation of young people as a way to change the world – that's in the next chapter. However, they do establish the fact that collaborations with children can be artistically viable and of interest to an adult contemporary-art audience. These examples, in fact, all predate the idea of the full participation of children, which really begins with the work that happened outside the auspices of Parkdale Public School, once the young people entered their teens. However, the projects here should be understood as decent examples of an aesthetic of civic engagement, the central idea presented in *Social Acupuncture*, published a month before the premiere of *Haircuts by Children*. Additionally, this bundle of projects, and my experience and that of my colleagues, can function as a case study both for working with children and for a socially engaged practice in general, particularly for artists interested in the very unartistic question of replicability – much more a concern for scientific inquiries – where the goal is to search for regularities and tease out successful causal mechanisms to reproduce them in other contexts with other populations.

Further, this work offers a rare look at an artistic engagement that is of unusually long duration and depth and that grew complex systems and relationships between the people and organizations. As a case study, or template, I hope the insights here have elements of context independence, which can be applied to other situations of long-term engagement, not necessarily with children and the cultural sector as targets.

The context-independent mechanism in this case is the simple but challenging-to-implement idea of sticking with particular populations for long periods of time and facilitating a range of encounters that invite these populations to adopt a wide variety of roles within the intervention, encountering each other in several different ways. Such an approach is likely to produce unexpected and surprising outcomes and trigger a rethinking and a *'rebeing'* of the particular populations and their relationships. I bring this up just to flag the idea that, whether the reader has an interest in collaborating with children or not, long-term engagement that comes from many different angles is a powerful tool for discovering things about the world that have simply not – and ordinarily would not – enter our minds.

Over the course of two years, Mammalian created fourteen projects with the young people of Parkdale Public School (detailed descriptions can be found in Appendix 1). Some were one-offs, while others had multiple iterations – in all, there were twenty-three distinct events, all primarily in Parkdale, including a two-week video shoot in the school itself, for an average of about one event a month. These events brought together over six hundred children from the school, a bunch of the teachers, about sixty artists, two dozen businesses and other local institutions, and thousands of audience members (*Ballroom Dancing* alone, a part of the first Nuit Blanche in 2006, drew over ten thousand). The audiences included other artists, the kids' parents and siblings, teachers, and the general public.

The work received a lot of attention from the media, producing an even wider audience, even as people might not have attended in person. While *Haircuts by Children* is best experienced in person, the concept itself is succinct and evocative enough to have an impact as merely an idea. For this reason, we summarized many of the projects in a series of posters designed by Cecilia Berkovic and Michael Barker that served as art objects and created another moment for an audience to encounter the work.

The work engaged the children and the public in a variety of ways. Some of these were very public, while others brought together only the young people and artists at the school and were designed to create connections well away from public scrutiny.

The projects can be sorted into different types by their various foci:

- collaborating artistically in a professional context with children
- connecting the children and local artists
- introducing the children to Mammalian's local audience
- connecting the children to local cultural institutions
- connecting the children and local businesses
- introducing the children to new art and ideas

For the most part, youth engagement is primarily – sometimes exclusively – concerned with the final focus: introducing young people to new art and ideas, with the goal being the children's edification, and typically does not consider the benefits to the wider community, the cultural sector, or local businesses. Highlighting the positive outcomes for the broader idea of the social fabric of the city, with the triggering of awareness – and possibly friendships – between young people and the adults is rare, but was, and remains, central to Mammalian's method.

This thinking is influenced primarily by the ideas of French sociologist Pierre Bourdieu, particularly the concepts of *social capital*, *cultural capital*, and *habitus*. The initiative was designed to build social capital – useful friendships – as well as sharing and developing cultural capital – basic knowledge of the cultural landscape, particularly knowledge of and access to the events and good times happening in our neighbourhood under the banner of creativity, arts, and culture. This was all intended to contribute to developing our – both the adults' and youths' – embodied disposition toward the world, our habitus, so that we all proceeded as changed people, emboldened and fortified by everything we had gained through the encounter.

For the children, this boiled down to sharing with them an understanding and embodied comprehension of the urban cultural fabric that Mammalian and our collaborators occupied so the young people could walk through Parkdale confident that they are not only welcome in the various institutions popping up as gentrification takes hold but also that they are, to some small degree, a *part* of these institutions. In terms of the effects on the various adult collaborators and audience, the work was intended to help us – as people who tend to live on the surface of the city, in relatively uniform groups who look like us and think like us – widen our perspectives and deepen our participation in the civic life of the city. Again, in contrast to most youth engagement, the beneficiaries of the work were both the children *and* the adults.

The initiative was developed to keep at least one eye solidly affixed to the long term, with the understanding that even the youngest child is only going to be a child very briefly and that there's no better time than the present to begin the process of building valuable social and professional networks, as well as to strengthen the children's sense of entitlement to participate in their changing neighbourhood. (*Entitlement* has become something of a swear word, but it's only an issue when that entitlement is not deserved, or earned. Young people *should* feel entitled to participate in the cultural landscape of the city, though often – especially in the case of racialized and marginalized populations – this participation is limited.)

Ultimately the projects were focused on social fortification, professional development, and network building; educational benefits to both the kids and the adults; and the creation of new and innovative work in collaboration with the kids.

The first and foremost intention was simply to *collaborate* with the children as artistic equals – which does not imply that the roles of the children and adults possess the same amount of power or control of the circumstances, but that the participation of the young people is not at all coercive, and that any direction provided by adults is up for discussion, subject to change, and consensual. This is no different than the typical relationship between a director and a performer who, when things are going well, always come to an agreement as to how a role is to be interpreted or, if disagreement persists, then they agree to disagree. As I mentioned in the first chapter, with children, unlike adults, there are far fewer opportunities to coerce them, if we proceed ethically. The bottom line is that, even if monetary compensation is offered – and with *Haircuts by Children* we do our best[51] to pay them – the children will not respond well, participate happily, or even remain on the project, if we don't manage to hold their interest. It is incumbent on us to provide activities that keep them coming back, rather than, as is often the case with activities intended to edify young people, keeping them there through force. To this end, then, one of the first rules of engagement is: no shushing. If what we're saying doesn't interest the young people, that's our problem, not theirs. A complete list of the various rules of engagement can be found in the Mammalian Protocol for Collaborating with Children, Appendix 2, which focuses on articles from the UN Convention on the Rights of the Child that are relevant to our practice.

The projects where artistic collaboration was central were *Haircuts by Children*; *Diplomatic Immunities: Life at Age Nine*; *Ballroom Dancing*; *The Children's Choice Awards*; *Walk the Block*; *Show and Tell*; *ADD DJS vs. LAL*; *The Kids' Table*; *The Parkdale Strings vs. Block Recordings Club*; *Shortcuts and Hangouts*; and *The Parkdale Art Club vs. Mercer Union.* The children's participation in these events, for the most part, did not demand much in terms of artistic rigour; they were involved as themselves, not as skilled performers, and this fact was central to the performances. So, for example, the craziness of the haircuts they gave in *Haircuts by Children*, their hilariously short attention span when it came to the task of DJing (which resulted in my dubbing their DJ collective the ADD DJs),[52] their unfiltered and often not so polite opinions during the *Children's Choice Awards*, and the awkward shyness they brought to the film *Show and Tell.*

The point with this particular work is not that we tend to underestimate the talents of children, though we often do, but that what children bring can, if framed properly, be as interesting as any well-rehearsed performance. Their presence, *as children*, is what conveys artistic significance, and not, as is often the case when people marvel at talented children, that they perform as well as adults. Some might – in fact, probably many can, with enough time and training – but regardless, children *as children* do offer artistic significance through their very presence.

When first conceived, *Haircuts by Children* was all about flipping hierarchies and trusting children with one of our most precious possessions: our vanity. It was a utopian proposition. In practice, the project expanded its meaning, leaving polemical intentions in the dust. As a performance, *Haircuts by Children* became much more about friendship, tenderness between strangers, and a momentary sense of belonging or community. With surprising consistency, the encounter between the young stylists and their relatively uniformly white art-hipster clients yields tender moments of intimacy and trust.

Following these insights, we developed two projects that looked specifically at the dynamic of this kind of intimacy, but this time over dinner. *The Beautiful Hungry City* (2007) was a City of Toronto–sponsored event that featured lectures by people who had jobs not ordinarily considered creative and who spoke about the beautiful aspects of their jobs. The event was attended by some of Toronto's hippest culturati, as well as children from Parkdale Public School and their parents, and everyone sat and ate together while listening to a firefighter, a paramedic, a flight attendant, a café owner, a court translator, and a few other professionals discussing the creative aspects of their work. *Eat the Street* (2008), which continues to tour, features a jury of children dining at a dozen restaurants over the course of a month. The children perform as food critics; for the price of a meal, the adult audience eats with the jury and spends time getting to know them. With *Eat the Street*, both adults and children are forced to deal head-on with social discomfort across an intergenerational divide. The preparatory work with the young people includes a look at the art of conversation: how to sustain small talk with people you don't know, don't share many interests with, and to whom you might not be able to relate.

In addition to creating interesting collaborations and artistic outcomes, this intimacy is designed to build significant and lasting connections between the young people, the artistic community, Mammalian's audience, and local businesses. A number of projects also addressed the question through other artistic forms. *Diplomatic Immunities: Life at Age Nine*, was a stage-based performance that brought a team of artists into the school to interview a class about what life is like at nine years old, with one of the students, Camille Balda, showing up at the performance at Buddies in Bad Times Theatre and joining us onstage. With the *Children's Choice Awards*, a jury of eleven children evaluated all the work at Alley Jaunt, a weekend-long art show happening in the garages surrounding Trinity Bellwoods Park, and then invited their favourite artists to a dinner sponsored by chef Nathan Isberg at his restaurant, Coca. (Isberg went on to do several other projects with the youth.)

Through these projects there is also the goal of introducing the young people to the cultural institutions and businesses in the neighbourhood, to the benefit of both parties, with the businesses and organizations encouraged to see these children as potential collaborators, customers, members, and participants, and the children asked to recognize that not only are they welcome in these venues, but their presence is *needed*. With *Eat the Street*, it is exciting to see restaurants taking the competition so seriously: the Drake Hotel, a venue often blamed for causing the gentrification in the neighbourhood, really raised the bar with their incredibly lavish treatment of the young people, who experienced an immediate spike in their cultural capital – *they had had dinner at the Drake.*

The program theory with *Eat the Street* and the *Children's Choice Awards* in particular is that the deleterious effects of gentrification or marginalization might, to a small degree, be tempered by the welcome offered by these businesses and institutions. Both projects now tour extensively, with each new locale featuring a jury of young people from the area, with restaurants and cultural institutions the young people would be unlikely to frequent invited to collaborate.

Perhaps it is delusional utopianism, but we've delivered this work in some allegedly challenging circumstances, including Molenbeek, the predominantly Moroccan neighbourhood in Brussels, which infamously produced the Paris and Belgium bombers. While its problems – exclusion from the Belgian job market and the wider Belgium society – are much too daunting for a piddly little art project, there is still the hope that dragging a bunch of children around to some of the city's most vibrant and venerated cultural institutions, where they are welcomed with abundant applause, will produce the understanding that they are appreciated, and welcome and loved. It might not be much, but maybe baby steps create small degrees of change that will produce a phase shift somewhere down the line.

On the adults' side, there is the hope that attitudes will shift, and people will begin to understand the youths, their families, and their neighbourhoods in a different way. A director of a European festival who had just moved to a famously rough neighbourhood populated primarily with Muslim families told us that spending time with the crew of ebullient children hailing from the same area had reduced the nervousness he felt when passing groups of teenagers on the street. It was a small but important win.

The community that emerged from this first phase of working with Parkdale Public School was ephemeral, and it's hard to say if it had any reality beyond the time we spent together. Maybe it was real, maybe it triggered people other than the company's closest associates to think differently about the city and the neighbourhoods we all share, maybe it bolstered the children's sense of their belonging in their own neighbourhood and therefore fostered a different relationship with the businesses, and maybe it created moments that had a meaningful and longer-term effect on people's lives. But maybe it didn't.

There are a few things I can say with certainty. First, the project created an environment favourable to a deeper engagement, which began in earnest in 2010 and continues today, which I address in the next chapter. Second, the attention the work received and continues to receive has been part of a growing international engagement with the idea of creating work in collaboration with children. There are now regular public and industry discussions that directly address this question.[53] Finally, the international touring life of many of the projects has meant that some of these ideas are continuing to spread as, ten years later, *Haircuts by Children, Eat the Street*, and the *Children's Choice Awards*, along with several other projects, remain in Mammalian's touring repertoire.

Though education and curricular support were not among the goals of the work with Parkdale Public School, these are important to consider, because without some nod to them, collaborating with schools is tough, if not impossible. The final part of this chapter is directed more toward artists and other practitioners, focusing on practical questions of engaging with schools as gatekeepers that most artists who work with young people are going to have to someday deal with.

In UNESCO's 2010 report *Arts Education for All: What Experts in Germany Are Saying*, Winfried Kneip, the director of the Centre for Education at the Mercator Foundation – the primary funder of Mammalian's long-term work at the Ruhrtriennale Festival in Germany – discusses the challenges of collaborating with schools, noting that what tends to be produced strays from the preferred outcomes of both artists and educators but can find common ground: 'art may be effective in the core area of education – if we succeed in defining a "curriculum of the imponderable," a third space, where art and school can meet.' As this suggests, the world of art and the world of school are not particularly compatible, and any comprehensive collaboration between artists and educators will need the understanding on both sides that we're creating something that can't fully satisfy either group's requirements.

Kneip observes, 'The culture of artists has not been able to influence the core of education, as determined by the "major subjects" such as ... language learning, mathematics and science.' Artists working on projects in collaboration with schools often fail to take into consideration the various deliverables that constrain teachers – primary among them that their emphasis must be on these major subjects. In fact, it's not unusual for those running the education and outreach departments of theatres, galleries, and festivals to have a vocal contempt for the formal education system, and sometimes they make the mistake of assuming that all teachers share this contempt. There are certainly some teachers who do, but many believe strongly in the education system. I've heard artists mock formal schooling to a teacher's face without the slightest recognition that it could be construed as an insult.

Kneip reports on a series of three yearly congresses to answer the following questions: In what ways can artists help educators effectively with their educational responsibilities? In what areas is it all too overwhelming or out of place for artists? To what extent can artists service education while maintaining artistic standards?

Each year of the congress focused on three different players: educators, artists, and children. Educators found that artists tend to make more work for the teachers, even when they are leading the activities, and that when artists introduce uninvited transformative processes into the school, they are often kicked out. For artists, the school is a not-always-comfortable place, often filled with bureaucracy and moral panic over the safety of the children. Kneip points out, 'Only artists who "use" schools within the very constraints they impose can claim to be acting in schools in an artistic mode.' Which means that, for the most part, artists are *not* wholly in an artistic mode while working with a school, which can be tough for the artists, as they have to conform to outcomes and evaluative measures they may not agree with, care about, or, for that matter, fully understand. Further, with respect to the children, they found that 'there are very few topics and few artistic processes which are not accessible to children,' so any artist that tries to gear their practice toward children by dumbing it down runs a risk of not being taken seriously by the kids; children pretty much get it all, no matter how baffled it might leave their teachers, and this can also create conflict.

Kneip makes a number of recommendations:

- Both teachers and artists need to be understood as experts in their field – as opposed to teachers being seen as not good artists and artists as not good teachers.
- Not only the students, but teachers, too, should be the focus of artistic activities.
- Artistic activities should not be pushed off into an area outside class.
- Artists need to be able to contribute learning that might not be valued by the school system.
- Artists must consider their work in terms of learning, even as that learning may be atypical and not something the artists have particularly valued.
- Artists require the support of experts in the pedagogy of arts and education, who are rare individuals.
- We all need to understand that artists who collaborate with schools are not failures, their work in education not a reluctant Plan B when the fame and fortune of Plan A doesn't materialize. Therefore, artists working in and with schools need to subject their work to the same high aesthetic standards they would if they were creating work with a team of adult professionals for a paying adult audience.

But why should artists bother to work with schools at all, particularly if educational outcomes are not of primary interest and we're more focused on aesthetic outcomes and productive collaborative relationships? This is an important question and, for the most part, it comes down to a single practicality: access – and, in particular, access to diversity. As ubiquitous as children might seem, they are *very difficult* to recruit for significant periods of time. The only places where children and adults spend any real time together is in the family and at school. Arts programs offered to youth in public community centres, privately, or through theatres or art galleries, for example, are another area to access children, but the children involved in those programs tend to be quite uniform: they're already interested in the arts, already have many assumptions about what art is, and often come from a position of some privilege.

With schools, artists can access a representative cross-section of the population, and if the artist is looking for a specific demographic – young people who come from marginalized communities, for example – then schools are often the only way to work with them. Compounding this is the fact that the education and outreach departments of most organizations, like galleries or performing arts festivals, tend to be under-resourced in relation to the rest of the organization and don't have the capacity to gather large groups of young people without some intermediary, like a school.

Our experience with *Parkdale Public School vs. Queen Street West,* as well as the work with schools around the world, has been very much in line with the insights of Kneip and bear repeating in the context of this collaboration. What follows are a few of the key points we took away from the residency and we now try to rigorously apply to the component projects as they tour. These are the absolutely necessary things that artists need to keep in mind when collaborating with a school.

1. *Do not* exclude the teachers. They will get huffy, if not downright nasty, and this is something we've had to learn again and again in many contexts, even as it's really hard to implement, particularly when touring a project, where the Mammalian team might show up just one day before we meet the teacher and the children. Artists need to understand that they are a potential threat to teachers, functioning as we often do like the hip aunt or uncle who can drop by, do some cool stuff, then just as quickly slip out. Teachers are there for the long haul, and it is easy for them to fall into the role of bad cop to the good cop of the artist. Perhaps counterintuitively, the teachers most likely to be threatened are the cool ones, those who've staked their identity on being slightly different than the stuffy teachers, as well as those

who teach the arts, who are more vulnerable to feeling undermined. Artists are just dropping by for a moment and do not carry the burden of assuring high test scores or policing certain behaviour, responsibilities that don't help the teacher win popularity contests with the kids. Artists must be sensitive to this.

2. Irony is not universal. Irony, these days one of the most highly valued of artistic currencies, is not something that is shared by everyone, particularly school administrators, who need to keep both the school board and parents happy. This careless and stupidly flippant statement on a poster we designed to promoted the project with Parkdale Public School got us into an understandable conflict with the school and we had do a completely new print run ($$!):

> In one corner, the kids, 647 of them. A massively diverse crew obsessed with PlayStation, teddy bears, fairness, and running the world. In the other corner: Artsters, predominantly white, mostly from other provinces and cities, well-educated in cultural theory, ready and eager to get drunk at gallery openings and always on the lookout for exciting but cheap ethnic dining experiences.

There were two concerns with this poster: the reference to getting drunk, which was thought to suggest that the kids would be chilling with the artists while they were actually inebriated; and that artists were well educated in cultural theory, which was thought to suggest that the kids at the school were not well educated.

That there was a mismatch in the appreciation of irony is obvious, and I don't think the problem needs further explication. If you must go with irony, bury it deep, or make it silly.

3. Stay away from journalists. Journalists need a story, a key component in a story is conflict, and school administrators don't find conflict particularly relaxing.

4. If at all possible, work directly with the parents, make a contract with them, and take full responsibility for the children's safety.

Some schools will welcome this and happily step aside, allowing the building to be used as a place for recruitment or meeting. Parents generally do not possess anywhere near the level of fear that a school administration has in dealing with so many competing interests. Parents are mostly interested in one thing: that their kids have a good time, which assumes they are safe and healthy while on the project. By and large, they don't care about too much else. As long as the kids are coming home with glowing reports of the amazing time they're having, parents will be onside.

Following this intense burst of activity from 2006 to 2008, much of it in collaboration with Parkdale Public School, Mammalian focused on touring the work internationally, taking a number of the projects on the road and realizing them around the world with local children.

4

CHILDREN VS. MAMMALIAN DIVING REFLEX

On June 28, 2010, while presenting *Haircuts by Children* at the London International Festival of Theatre in the gentrifying neighbourhood of Canning Town, I received a Facebook message from Sanjay Ratnan, a fourteen-year-old Toronto kid who had worked on *Eat the Street* two years earlier. He was looking for a venue to showcase his singing. A month later, back in Toronto, we met at the Parkdale Burger King. Sanjay brought along his cousin, Gobika Karunanithi, who had also worked on *Eat the Street*, and a new kid, Kathy Vuu, who introduced herself as a dancer. I brought along Tenzin Chosang, who had also worked on *Eat the Street* and whom I had bumped into the day before while he waited for a bus outside my apartment. Chosang dragged along his friend Tenzin Chozin. Together, we all agreed to make a film.

We spent one day shooting random stuff near Parkdale Public School, as well some footage along the train tracks at Dufferin and Queen Streets, mostly shots of them throwing rocks against the wall that separates the tracks from West Lodge, a large apartment complex where many of the Parkdale kids live, with repeated appearances on lists of the city's worst landlords. During the shoot, Chozin took a photo in which Chosang appeared to be levitating, with West Lodge clearly in the background.

Using the photo as the centrepiece, I wrote a short script about an exhausted travelling salesman, played by Sanjay, who finds a photograph of one of his team levitating. Convinced the levitation trick is their ticket to fame and fortune – and, in turn, a way to stop all the arduous travel – the salesman tries to get his employee to reproduce the magic, but the guy's stage fright is too severe and the film ends with the salesman heading back on the road. The film, titled simply *The Torontonians*, was conceived as a series that I would shoot with the youth, but my ineptitude with editing forced us back

onto familiar terrain: performance. (I will get to the film eventually. As I recall, we did an okay job. The footage sits on a hard drive somewhere.) Over the fall of 2010, Sanjay recruited a small ensemble of his friends to round out the collective, which we agreed to name the Torontonians, and we began a collaboration that continues today. With this small film, the very beginnings of a method for working with young people started to take shape: creative play driven by the youth that produces small whiffs of content – in this case, a random photo – around which I construct a form. Over the following years, we developed many more projects, including formalizing the very method used to yield these projects: the Succession Model of Youth Labour Engagement (the SMYLE).

This methodology for youth engagement is probably my most convincing evidence that young people can be involved with an organization at deeper levels, including program development and delivery, and that their participation in all matters affecting them can have positive outcomes for themselves, the surrounding adults, and the organization itself. By extension, this is also some of the best evidence I have for the viability of a new social contract with young people in general.

The organic emergence of this approach could not have happened without the youth, but it is important to understand that we didn't sit down around a boardroom table and hash it all out on a whiteboard. It was developed in opposition to the tyranny of strategic planning, which, while useful in circumstances where the parameters are locked in, offers much less when you're looking for innovation. Even the best strategic planning has one huge limitation: our experience. What we imagine is possible tends to be constrained by what we already understand, and by what has already been possible. Had Mammalian in 2006 strategized and defined goals for the subsequent ten years, there is absolutely no way we would have settled on anything as ridiculous as conceiving, developing, implementing, and propagating an approach to working with young people that advocated for a wholesale overhaul of society to include the participation of youths in all matters affecting them, let alone this idea as a revolutionary proposal intended to intervene in worldwide social and economic relations. Instead, *emergent* planning is a better way to describe how the youth and our team collaborated to create the smyle. Collaboration with children, then, not only yielded a method of working with children, but it yielded the method to yield this method.

Emergent planning came about because of what might ordinarily be described as the *limitations* of the young people: their short attention, their weak understanding of longer time spans – an absolute necessity for strategic planning – and their meagre experience of and interest in the minutiae of youth mentorship. When these limitations are reclassified as assets and we focus on the traits they *do* bring to the table – playfulness, irrationality, unfiltered expression of feelings, an ability to blissfully ignore the stifling dictates of professionalism – we increase our chances of producing unusual, surprising, and groundbreaking strategies. The development of the smyle itself should be understood as evidence that including young people in the process of program development can produce unexpected but powerful results, provided the kids' natural tendencies are not seen as liabilities.

The sort of planning that emerged has applications for situations that do not involve young people; it can be applied widely and in an increasing variety of circumstances. As I stated earlier, the world of work is evolving rapidly in ways that allow for the fuller participation of young people, and, in fact, children are already present and driving innovation there. The simple example of learning to use a new piece of software illustrates the wider changes in the world. Even the most workaday software, like Microsoft Word, is too complex for the old-school approach of reading a manual cover-to-cover before settling down to use the product. Instead, some combination of curious exploration, the constant querying of myriad formal and informal websites, advice from friends and colleagues, communication with the software's technical support staff, and repeated trial and error is the only way to master these applications. This approach is inherently childlike: curiosity, constantly asking question after question, and relentlessly trying different approaches. This is starkly opposed to rationally parsing the situation and then systematically and linearly acquiring the skills – which could be considered more adult-like. (These two descriptions are stereotypes, but the very concepts of child and adult are themselves stereotypes.)

The biggest difference is that children simply do not have a repertoire of experience to refer to, experience that can have the effect of locking a person into attempting only strategies that have worked before. This was not a problem in the relatively recent past, when the technologies that reproduced daily life were part of long traditions where knowledge was preserved and passed from one generation to the next. These days, things are so complex, and change at such high speeds, that the old forms of knowledge generation and transfer, and the more rational management and strategic planning approaches, do not yield the necessary innovations.

Children simply do not like to spend time in meetings planning for futures that don't exist and are impossible to predict. Further, they quite naturally reject the absurd and impossible idea that the workplace should be a site of pure rationality where pesky things like boredom, interests, social norms, or candour are sidelined via bureaucratic totalitarianism by those terrified of the messiness of their own hearts. Children are experts at breaching stale professionalism, they bring chaos to the best-laid plans, and they are not afraid to ask awkward questions and say uncomfortable truths. Working with young people to produce program innovation is as rewarding as it is challenging, but it is not a gig for cowards.

In this chapter I introduce the SMYLE, itemizing the various principles, explaining how they fit together in a cohesive whole, and how they can potentially bring young people deep into an organization, where they are able to participate and then, eventually, assume control – the logical end game of any comprehensive mentorship.

The kids from the Parkdale Public School project who became a part of the SMYLE are all the children of immigrants, if not immigrants themselves, from countries outside of the European/U.K. nexus and colonial diaspora. So the method that emerged is particularly well suited to situations where a population of young people is underrepresented within a wider homogeneous environment. The common shorthand for these young people is 'marginalized,' a concept that does them a disservice, bundled as it is with the idea of poverty. When an outside expert is hired to enter any environment, to assess it and offer recommendations, they, too, occupy a marginal position; we think of this kind of marginalization as an advantage, with their external perspective giving them power. However, this power only works if there's buy-in from those at the centre. Marginalized youth occupy a similarly powerful vantage point, which also gives them expertise, whether they know it or not, allowing them to perceive the machinations of institutional and social power, and the inequities within society, which can be difficult for those at the centre to see, let alone admit. The difference between the expert and the so-called marginalized child is that, in children, this expertise is not recognized as such – a straightforward problem of racism and ageism.

Part of the effectiveness of the SMYLE, then, derives from recognizing and deploying this expertise, which creates a reciprocity that drives the method, making it much more useful than mere altruism: we're not here to make the lives of the poor, disadvantaged kids better, we're here to make the lives of *everyone* better. This involves recognizing the *disadvantage* of those of us occupying more central positions, who may have more access to more resources but have a hampered perception of social realities due to a collective effort to shield ourselves from the facts. (A few honest conversations with youth of colour about their day-to-day experience can provide a small glimpse of the kind of knowledge that eludes the perception of those of us who are not of colour.)

So, not only was the method developed with young people – a population always in a marginal position in relation to adults – but also with particular young people who have an acute and embodied sense of the inequities of their world in general and the cultural sector surrounding them in particular. It is this double marginalization that makes the method particularly powerful. It doesn't need both marginalizations to be in place, however: the method can also work with a bunch of privileged kids, *and* with a bunch of marginalized *adults*.[54] But at this point, I will stick to discussing its application within a youth-engagement framework, one interested in addressing social inequities that tend to break down around race, ethnicity, culture, or whichever limited short-hand is used to describe the problem.

I turn again to the case study of the artistic and creative work in Toronto that the youth and I engaged in, out of which the model emerged and that provides examples of it in action as it was assembled and refined. This portion of the case study looks at the years 2010 to 2014, when the bulk of the young people were fourteen to eighteen years old, had graduated from Parkdale Public School, and were enrolled at the nearby Parkdale Collegiate Institute, though we did not collaborate with the latter school. Additionally, though they unfolded organically and were not strategically developed as such, these four years of work in Parkdale formed a logical and step-wise youth engagement program that responded to their needs and wishes, crystallizing and yielding an approach with the potential for replication. Again, this is a testament to the power of the method, in that our attentive response to the needs of the young people, though not at all carefully rationalized and planned, ended up producing a cohesive whole, which, after the fact, *appears* to have been carefully plotted.

The SMYLE is an approach to working with young people that attempts to flatten hierarchies through the primary principle of succession and, following succession, a cascading series of logically following secondary principles, including collegiality, the division of labour, the production and sharing of social capital, friendship, low numbers/high impact, and performativity. Though we developed it under the auspices of a performance company, the model is applicable in a wide range of contexts and organizations. These could be theatre companies, art galleries, festivals of all sorts, a variety of social-justice-related organizations, organizations concerned with civic engagement, urban-planning initiatives, local government, social service provision, the media, community centres, and community service organizations, as well as small businesses or large corporate entities, which tend to already feature high school placements, co-ops, and other similar programs. In short, it is difficult to imagine many contexts and organizations that would not, to some degree, be amenable to the model.

The SMYLE's grounding assumption, reflected in the use of the word *labour* in the method's name, is that the time the youth spend engaged in activities with the organization is understood as *work*, even as it might serve an educational purpose – education itself is arguably another form of work. But, while work, it is not 'child labour,' with its suggestion of exploitation, and does not resemble the harmful activities that concern the International Labour Organization, mentioned earlier.

There's no doubt the youths' work with Mammalian is a series of activities that produce value, some of which is captured by the youth, some by Mammalian, some by me, some by the various organizations my company works with, and some by others, provisionally described by the shorthand 'society,' which benefits from some of the positive effects generated by a bunch of teens producing a bunch of performances and activities about their reality.

The SMYLE, to some extent, relies on accepting that the division between work and 'life' has dissolved;[55] that volunteering, socializing, playing, working, and engaging in civic responsibilities often blend into each other; and that investments in one area can produce value in the others. While this situation has rallied many people to push back with a focus on life/work balance, in some instances – particularly in sectors that themselves produce elements of leisure, like arts and culture – it is difficult to establish this balance. At its most faithful application, the SMYLE attempts to reckon with the dissolving of this division between life and work, accepting it as a challenging fact of the contemporary world of work. But on the upside, as a model for transformation, it has the advantage of also affecting the lives of the practitioners delivering the strategy, who are also targets of the intervention, as their personal lives are also a site of the intervention. If this were not the case, the model would be based on altruism – which maintains a power imbalance – and not on meaningful social change, which, ideally, addresses imbalance.

The goal is not to fight to maintain something, such as work/life balance, which, by the sector's very nature, is next to impossible, but rather to attempt to *infuse work itself with more life*, shifting the idea of balance to a different register. This shift occurs by including children in work as agents of life, where the work/life balance will always be decided in favour of life. Children can be mobilized against the infiltration of life by work since, even as we bring them into them into the world of work, they bring their capacities to physically resist boredom and to engage in play, for example – they bring a civil disobedience by being themselves. In the context of working with young people, things begin to look a little like family. It is a natural by-product of the development of friendships that occur when the boundary between work and life is dissolved, and this lends the model its powerful social cohesiveness. The ask of the SMYLE is high, but so are the rewards and, whether or not you are able to reach for the full utopian hallucination and believe that flooding as much of our world with the presence of children can have a positive effect on social relations across all realms, you can at least rest assured the implementation will net you a whole bunch of new great friends.

I know that taking key principles from our work in Parkdale and implying that the model is replicable in other contexts falls more on the side of science than art, where the focus is very much on difficult-to-reproduce originality. But I'm trying to have my cake and eat some sushi, too: these principles are designed to fall somewhere between art and science, offering enough guidance to reproduce aspects of the success in Parkdale, while remaining flexible enough to yield different activity outcomes, whatever those activities might be – in Mammalian's case, art. Developing activities in collaboration with youth is the short-term and non-negotiable goal of the SMYLE, with the long-term goal being succession. Unlike programming, though, succession is understood to be a future – even utopian – target, but a target that shapes the terms of the engagement in the present. What follows are the key principles of the SMYLE, interwoven with the case study of the work with the Torontonians. (I will refer to the various projects to support my case, but won't spend too much describing them, leaving that to Appendix 1, where I go into detail.)

Succession

The SMYLE flows logically from the straightforward idea that the work with the youth is geared toward succession: the youth's eventual assumption of control of the company, as those leading the organization mentor the young people and expand their own activities to other areas to make space for these future leaders. This should be distinguished from the idea of youth-led – or, as it is called in the U.K., peer-led – projects where young people are given hived-off responsibilities that usually remain outside the organization's primary activities, occurring off in the youth wing. This is not to say these sorts of programs don't have an important impact on the young people, but this kind of engagement is not intended to have an equal and commensurate impact on the organization running the program; it is not designed to change the organization's contours.

Room to Rise: The Lasting Impact of Intensive Teen Programs in Art Museums is a comprehensive 2015 study of the impact of four of America's most notable youth engagement programs: the Whitney Museum's Youth Insights, New York; the Walker Center's Teen Arts Council, Minneapolis; the Contemporary Arts Museum's Teen Council, Houston; and the Museum of Contemporary Art's MOCA Mentors, Los Angeles. The study's framework is focused almost exclusively on the impacts that these programs have had on the lives of the young participants, with twelve of the programs' alumni presented as case studies. While the chapter 'Changing Museums' does examine the effects these programs have had on the institutions themselves, these effects are not – unlike the effects on the youth – examined at the level of individuals, with no case studies provided for the impacts on the adults at these institutions. Instead the study presents the aggregate learnings that benefitted the organization as a whole. These are primarily changes of attitudes toward audience development, with the common takeaway that teens are 'a natural audience for contemporary art' and that the youth influenced the way the museum sought and welcomed diverse audiences, managing to, not surprisingly, attract other teens. They also found that the museums began to see the value in other perspectives and to develop more diverse sets of programming, which, while clearly important is, again, like audience development, an outward-facing concern and was consistently tied back to building audience with the logic that new types of programming mean new types of customers.

The findings of *Room to Rise* are certainly good news, and the youth programs clearly had a positive impact on both the youth and the museums; however, what was missing was any evidence that this impact and change occurred to the individuals *running* the organizations or the inner machinations of the organization itself. Beyond broadening minds about the potential of building more diverse audiences, there was no discussion of any reciprocal impact on the way the museums themselves function, which can, therefore, be assumed to be minimal.

The idea of succession as central to any youth-engagement framework, on the other hand, forces these considerations into the foreground, as the organization itself and *the very individuals within it* must grapple with how exactly things will change in response to the presence of the young people, well beyond the limited concern of expanding programming. Without succession, the institutions are shielded from more drastic impact and change, which may go a long way toward explaining why, after years and years of hand-wringing, the sector remains frustratingly homogeneous, with this question of minimal diversity still prominent and unsolved on the agenda.

An obvious objection to the idea of succession is feasibility: it is not realistic to expect that all the young people who are engaged will be hired, let alone want to work for a given organization. But that's okay; the ideal of secession is just that, an ideal. It should be taken seriously but it does remain a goal – a utopian target that we may or may not hit to greater or lesser degrees. However, proceeding *as if* this goal were possible changes the orientation to all the organization's activities as we attempt to align many of the activities toward the participation of the youth.

Specifically within the arts and cultural sector, youth engagement is now almost exclusively focused on developing artistic skills, while whole vast submerged portions of cultural organizations are not considered, let alone offered to the youth as possible sites for mentorship and learning. Recently, I used the SMYLE as a framework to assess the Art Gallery of Ontario, an institution with an annual budget of over $70 million, and found that the youth recruited to serve on the gallery's youth council knew almost nothing about anything other than the education and curatorial departments. There was little awareness of the function of other massive and crucial areas, including Marketing and Publicity, Public Affairs, Visitor Experience, Membership Services, Operations, Development, Finance, Food and Beverage, and Preservation and Protection. There is nothing unusual about this, and I assume most other museums' youth-engagement programs would yield the same finding.

Once the young people met and interviewed a few of the directors of these departments, they remarked that there was much more to the gallery than they had expected, and that many of the jobs were of interest. This also came as a surprise to many of these department directors, who assumed that artistic creation and curating were the only things young people cared about. The directors thought their jobs were too boring for the young people, underestimating both the youth and the creative interest of these jobs. With succession, these departments would be considered to potentially include the participation of young people, thus drastically expanding the impact of the organization's youth engagement and mentorship potential. As an example from Mammalian, although we've been hiring the youth for short-term project-oriented work since the beginning, our first long-term hire was Isabel Ahat, one of the young people we've been working with the longest, who is studying accounting and was hired as an accounting assistant; she is currently expanding her role to include production and creation. That accounting would be the first long-term gig we offered to a young person could not have been predicted, but, responding to her interest, it made the most sense. When people in the arts talk about youth engagement, they're usually not talking about engaging the kids in the finance department, but maybe they should.

With the idea of succession in place, a cascade of other principles logically follow, all of which have, over the last seven years with the Parkdale youth, had the sort of reciprocal impact that the idea of succession implies. First of all, structuring and conceiving of all the organization's activities with the intention of succession yields a particular orientation to the youth: collegiality, the SMYLE's second principle.

Collegiality

Succession implies that the young people working with the company are, in fact, our colleagues, which means the work we create must be equally important to both parties and have the potential to affect all of our lives. This statement is often met with resistance; people point to the power imbalance between the adults and the young people, and the fact that the young people are in a weaker position and therefore not our colleagues. But I'm not suggesting we are somehow equal, an impossibility even between adult collaborators; we all have different skills and different positions from which to exert leverage, even up and down hierarchies. People objecting to my approach to the young people as colleagues make an assumption similar to the one that the liberal rational subject is the legitimate universal subject. Instead, in the case of the SMYLE, let us think of the universal subject as Fineman's vulnerable subject (introduced in the chapter 'Children vs. Capitalism'). What this means in practice is that we presuppose that *all* colleagues are vulnerable and *all* must be treated like children, which is to say: with care. But most work environments use a paradigm rooted in totalitarian professionalism, meaning that this doesn't happen. Collegiality with young people needs to be approached differently and with much more care than we currently have the courage and compassion to grant each other as adults.

One of the biggest areas in which the youth have a huge amount of power is in their decision to participate at all. As I've mentioned, children do not respond well to monetary rewards, which can never be large enough to keep them sitting still when they're bored, something I consider one of their most exciting skills: they are difficult to buy. This in contrast to adults, who've learned very well the tradeoff between making money and suffering boredom, the basics of which were taught through coercion in the school system. For children, such incentives simply do not work. As anyone who runs any kind of program for youth knows, recruitment and retention is not an easy task, and those who manage to keep the attention of youth for longer periods must be offering something the youth find valuable. Within a youth arts setting, this power to walk away evens the playing field, with the young people needing to feel they are being offered something of value.

Once we accept the fact that the young people are our colleagues, with whom we are creating work that, in the case of Mammalian, we're trying to peddle on the performing arts market, we introduce a dynamic that contains an element of selfishness – a block against altruism. This is not an accident, altruism being more inclined to reinforce current social imbalances than to correct them.[56] The model intentionally frustrates these impulses by situating concern for the company and my own personal future within the consideration of my collaboration with young people. Their interests are my interests and my interests are theirs; we sink or swim together.

With the question of collegiality, we also need to honestly examine the issue of exploitation in relation to the labour of the young people. Earlier, I made it clear that this collaboration is not the sort of child labour that needs to be eradicated. However, there is still David Oldman's idea of a generational mode of production and, in particular, childwork, where the activities of children are corralled and supervised by adults, for the benefit of the adults, in environments and situations that are not optimal for the kids. In our case, these performances with children seem fine: the kids have a great time, they are often paid (unless a gatekeeper, like a school admin-istration, objects), and there are educational and other pro-social outcomes, like confidence, self-assurance, experiencing new things, etc. However, when applying another of Oldman's tests – if the children's participation is removed, do the adults suffer a reduction in their benefits? – the answer is a pretty resounding yes, as it is with compulsory schooling and daycare, and the value the teachers and caregivers capture. We couldn't have run these projects without them, and the company itself would not be where it is today without the labour of thousands of children we've collaborated with around the world. Therefore, the decision to focus on the Toronto youth as colleagues is motivated by the desire to 'give back,' to be absolutely certain that the value Mammalian is generating through this inter-national touring is shared with the young people with whom we devised this work.

In terms of the relationship with the Torontonians collective, the plan we came up with was to designate Toronto as their domain. With abundant opportunities to present and create work elsewhere in the world, the deal we made was that everything the company did in Toronto would, from that point on, in some way or another, and to the best of our ability, involve the Torontonians, whether that was a performance, a talk, or a panel. (As with any principle, rigidity is not always possible, but when we deviate from these prin-ciples, we know it.) This commitment to making Toronto the youths' realm is even stronger today, especially as international commitments demand more and more attention, exemplifying the idea that succes-sion does not imply bumping off the old guys, but that, as senior members of the team, it is our responsibility to diversify and expand our activities – it would have been more difficult for Mammalian to expand internationally without the kids holding down the fort at home. This is yet another corrective to altruism: the inclusion of the young people provides a path for organizational growth and change, further evidence that the relationship is collegial.

The question of collegiality brings up another set of issues around the ethics of the working relationship, particularly when we're making the lives of the young people the content of the work –

especially in our films, where we've mobilized biography to strong effect. This raises concerns about the ownership of the stories, which boils down to questions of what we are doing with the films and whether everyone is comfortable with their share of influence and compensation. With all the work, we offer full veto to the youth – they can, at any moment, drop out of a project with absolutely no repercussions, or ask that their footage be dropped. Sensitivity to changes in opinion about their participation is important and, though we've never encountered this, the power to veto future distribution of films must be a possibility.

As people whose position in the social landscape is marginal and whose power is often scant, children are frequently bossed around in ways that undermine the principles we try to adhere to, both in the SMYLE and in the Mammalian Protocol for Collaborating with Children. This bossing around can come from a variety of different stakeholders, but it tends to come from the institutions or individuals that are generously allowing us access to the children in the first place, whether that's a school or just a collection of parents. They are probably in the strongest position of all of us, certainly being more powerful than the children, Mammalian, our presenting partners, and me. They're the boss, and working with them in a spirit of collegiality can be a challenge. It is not unusual for the children and young people to want to do something within a project that is vetoed by the institutions we partner with. This can range from a joke they want to make during the *Children's Choice Award* ceremony, to the music they want to play in a hair salon during *Haircuts by Children*, to a tree they want to climb in *Nightwalks with Teenagers*.

A final issue for the principle of collegiality is competition and control over artistic process and product: achieving consensus is easier said than done. This means it's important to consider leadership style and certain traits when assigning people the task of leading a youth program. Artistic confidence is probably the most important trait. The leaders of youth arts initiatives need to be at a stage in their career at which they've reached a level of relaxed satisfaction and ease about their own artistic acheivments and do not need to prove themselves. While collegiality demands that the work should be important to the adults, proving oneself artistically while in consensus-based collaboration with children and young people is not easy, and making the mistake of competing with the kids is really not a good look. Related is the issue of those working within the youth arts sectors who make a distinction between their work with the youth and their 'real' practice, which they value more. The role of leading youth engagement under the banner of collegiality requires people with enough vision to perceive that time moves fast, the youth are only briefly youth, a thorough collaboration is being developed, and working with youth, as central to an artistic practice, is totally viable.

Collegiality might be the most challenging to apply in realms other than youth arts programming and is probably the most context-dependent of all the principles. In the arts, it is not so difficult to position young people as colleagues, but within other sectors, where there might be more profound and challenging implications – within firefighting or heart surgery, for example – it will likely be more difficult. In these cases, one should regard whatever contribution the young people do make with as much openness as possible, and constantly question whether this contribution can be positioned more centrally to the organization, always on the lookout for more meaningful activities as a central component of the mentorship or placement. This is, for the most part, how a good co-op placement or internship already works, so this principle is not so extreme. The key is to make this search for higher degrees of collegiality a primary part of the program.

Division of Labour

The principle of collegiality logically introduces the possibility of dividing up roles in a project to allow everyone to participate not only to the best of their ability but with an eye toward their particular expertise, however atypical that expertise might be – which, in the case of children, can be fairly atypical. (Who could forget Moe, a ten-year-old girl in Tokyo who can sculpt perfectly round human hairballs?) Expertise in this sense does not mean professional expertise or expertise learned through training but is, instead, an expertise in their own experience and expression as young people who occupy a certain place within the social structure and their own life trajectory. It can also be a creative expertise that many young people have easy access to, as they live their life in a constant state of play and expressive experimentation. For example, the photo taken by Tenzin Chozin of the levitating Tenzin Chosang was a random moment captured simply because, when working with young people, I try to always give them plenty of time with cameras, knowing that most photos won't be great, but some will be brilliant. Chozin's composition is fantastic: the odd skewing of the frame; Chosang's face illegible in the shadow of the tree, which we see cast on the ground below him; his headphone cord, which also seems to possess the power of levitation; West Lodge in the background; and a near pristine sky. None of this was planned, nor was the script I developed in response to the photo. In this way, young people, through both their presence and their intentional/accidental creative acts, often provide great, but relatively raw, content.

This raw content – and all artistic work starts with a pile of raw material, in one form or another – is then refined through the expertise that the adults are better positioned to bring: a formal understanding of the way things tend to work and, in the context of artmaking, how we can frame what we're doing as art; what we can get away with; and how to pitch it to interested partners. It is not natural for somebody to appreciate the fact that a urinal, a shark floating in formaldehyde, and an urban planning project to run a bakery[57] can all be pieces of art – each of these projects needed some framing to be regarded as art. Within artistic practice, then, form can loosely be considered the adults' domain, while content is the domain of the children. As collaborating adults, our biggest job is to observe carefully and focus on what is surprising, interesting, funny, charming, and revealing to us about the young people's activities and opinions.

Within the collaborations with the Torontonians, several projects demonstrate this principle particularly well, including *Nightwalks with Teenagers, High School Health*, and *Sleeping with Family*.

Nightwalks with Teenagers was conceived in response to the observation that, during social outings, the youth would vie to be dropped off last, fighting over the right to stay out a bit longer, wandering through the city at night. They managed to turn absolutely typical aspects of the urban landscape into a fun, complex playground, enjoying the freedom of exploring the city; the safety of the group – particularly the presence of adults – provided a platform for the youth to interact with the public that was very close to performance. To turn the whole thing into a performance was simply a matter of bringing in an understanding of form and making a few tweaks, so the spontaneous things that occurred once could be repeated. The adult audience became more than a typical group of spectators – they became co-performers, with the walk designed to be an adventure for *both* parties.

This is an instance of collegiality that also functions performatively. The wandering group is an unusual social configuration that is a reality for the moment of the performance and should attract attention and curiosity from passersby, and it should also trigger some questions: What is this odd, intergenerational, and (hopefully) intercultural group doing wandering through the city at night? Who are they? How did they meet? What is the purpose of their meanderings? The event should look like a new reality, suggestive of the generous possibilities of the social sphere that remain suppressed due to irrational fear and a hyper-vigilance that does more damage than good.

Mammalian's film projects, created in collaboration with Nicole Bazuin, serve as probably the best examples of a collegial relationship that sees a division in the labour between the creation of content and form, since filmmaking, by its very nature, makes that distinction clear.

The idea for our series of short films about love and dating, *High School Health*, was seeded in conversation with the then-fourteen-year-old Tenzin Chosang, Tenzin Chozin, and Ahash Jeeva. They wanted to discuss the new and confusing challenges they were just starting to face in the world of romantic relationships. I was surprised by my response to this inquiry. The deal was: I *really* wanted to help, but the sensitivity of the subject meant that my help had to be carefully considered. I didn't want to offer bad, frivolous, or otherwise ill-considered information. These small, casual sessions happened a few more times, and often included personal questions about my own experience, which I answered with as much honesty as I felt was appropriate. I began to jokingly refer to these moments as 'high school health class.'

I wanted other people to experience this sensation of being grilled about dating by a bunch of teens, where the desire to communicate with maximum generosity is irresistible, even at the expense of privacy – or rather, *especially* at the expense of privacy, again in a deployment of discomfort. I wanted to find powerful, confident people, put them in front of an audience, and have them field the prying, uncensored questions of a crew of teens who were just trying to figure out one of life's biggest mysteries: love.

I leveraged all the cultural capital I could muster and enlisted a crew of illustrious Toronto artists: broadcaster and novelist Ann-Marie MacDonald, novelist Wayson Choy, filmmaker Atom Egoyan, memoirist and Mammalian Diving Reflex performer Bette Logan, singer/songwriter Dan Hill, and actor Kim Roberts, who were interviewed by Virginia Antonipillai, Daniel Lastres Rodrigues, Sanjay Ratnan, Wendell Williams, and Kathy Vuu. These youth had distinguished themselves over the years as being most capable of asking prying questions, a skill some young people have a very good grip on. The adults, as predicted, stepped up with full generosity and shared painful, funny, and searingly honest details about their lives: terrible times and times of indescribable and incomprehensible joy, and, most interestingly and unexpected, plenty of evidence that there are many forms a family can assume beyond a mom, a dad, and the kids. The project was shot to appear as if the celebrity guest had just dropped by after school for a casual chat with a few young people who happened to be hanging around. These interviews were rounded out by individual interviews with the youth, who analyzed the adults and brought their own experience of human nature into the mix, trying to understand what might motivate some of the life choices they had just heard related.

Sleeping with Family is a short experimental documentary created in direct response to the close friendships we developed with the

Torontonians and their immediate group of friends. Over the years working with them, I was repeatedly surprised to learn about people's cramped living quarters; many of the kids lived in small Parkdale apartments with large families. I established two conditions for participation in the film: the youth either had to share a bedroom with at least a parent or sleep in a non-bedroom area of the home with a sibling. Because the subject was so sensitive, I promised the young people anonymity through the use of a witness-protection-style interview with backlighting and voice modulation, as if revealing their identity would put them in grave danger. In the end, they were pleased with the project and agreed to use their names in the credits.

There is a deep collegiality among the creative team and, together, we develop content for artistic consideration, paying careful attention to the lives and interests of the young people, while the adults bring their expertise to the minutiae of artmaking. But, ultimately, what these two principles produce is not such a big deal – it is really just plain old high-quality artistic collaboration, something that would seem utterly normal if not for the fact that the collaboration is intergenerational.

The applications of this division of labour are relatively obvious in the world of performance and particularly in socially engaged art, which is extremely flexible and accommodating of the interests of collaborators and participants. It is not as clear how this approach might be applied in other circumstances, where the activities of an organization may not be so easily wrapped around the natural expression of young people – such as a bank, for example. Like collegiality, this principle can be downgraded to more simply mean the obvious principle of taking into account the interests of one's colleagues or staff when designing or assigning tasks. If the intern at the design firm is a foodie, put her on the project about edible cookie dough. In this context, then, the principle is not particularly radical; in fact, it is a commonplace strategy to keep an eye on junior members of a team and to engage their interests and natural tendencies.

The other thing collegiality does is introduce the idea of a broader community, colleagues beyond the immediate circle of the organization. These are people and relationships that are important for the youth to have access to if the concept of collegiality is to be taken seriously. And this leads logically to the next principle: social capital.

Social Capital

Implied in the concept of collegiality is the idea of social capital, understood as the networks one is able to tap to produce value. Networks are central to many industries, particularly arts and culture, where jobs are more likely to flow from one's connections. If I am working with a colleague, it is also understood that the relationship includes sharing and building networks and fostering opportunities between us and our other collaborators.

The young people are important nodes within my professional network, and I make great efforts to connect them to my adult colleagues through the ancient art of socializing, the 'party' being my key methodological instrument. I constantly drag the youth to talks, openings, and friends' parties. Both the youth and my adult artist friends tend to remain in their own cliques, but friendships have developed, some of which continue today.

But if there is any controversial aspect to the model, it is this principle of *social capital*, which connects directly to the principle of *friendship*. But it's not insurmountable: the strategy for making sure everybody remains safe is to be totally transparent and ensure that there are always tons of people involved to maintain accountability.

The worry here is the same as with any youth group: the possibility of inappropriate or predatory behaviour. A common concern is that this setup could be an opportunity for grooming the youth for sexual relationships. Again, the key is the full participation of a whole lot of people, which increases the number of eyes on the project. But, of course, grooming is very sneaky, surreptitious, and historically has happened in full view of adults who didn't recognize the signs, refused to believe, or deliberately looked away.

How significant are the risks of this sort of thing in this particular context? It's very hard to say. Trying to tease out accurate data about the prevalence of child sexual abuse – let alone data that might be relevant to the SMYLE – is notoriously challenging. Some studies and journalists focus on the number of cases that have been *reported*, others deal only with *substantiated* cases, while still others recognize that the numbers reported or substantiated are going to underrepresent the problem, so they attempt to survey adults, asking if they've ever been sexually abused when they were young, whether or not the incident was reported.

But since one abused child is still way too many, rather than making any definitive attempt to decide the size of the risk one way or the other, a better course of action might be to increase efforts toward prevention through education and discussion, something the U.K. government has declined to do, despite the recommendation by four House of Commons committees.

A blanket prohibition against contact outside of the strict confines of the program is clearly a weakest-link approach, where everyone must act like all the adults are potential perpetrators. The question is straightforward: is a blanket prohibition really the best we can do? We're all creative people; I'm sure there's a better solution out there.

In the context of the SMYLE, a corrective that respects the intelligence of the young people might be to gather everybody together, including all the young people, their parents, and the mentoring adults, state clearly what the dangers are, decide together what behaviours are cool and which are not, identify indicators to watch out for, clearly outline how to respond to a threat, and enforce simple rules like a ban on an adult and a youth being alone for any significant length of time.

The problem with this: it's just not expedient.

To discuss these issues with all involved will require a ton of logistics and eat up the precious time spent on the program itself. And, beyond this practicality, it will be hellishly awkward. But, again, expediency is – across this entire proposal – something that must be jettisoned if we want to be serious about the participation of children across all realms affecting them.

While even a single child abused is too many, there may be unintended negative consequences generated by very high levels of child protection that, in the end, cause even more harm. Does the vociferous policing of the association between adults and young people produce a world that is safer for children, whose access to trusted adults is hampered?

The U.K. is a special case, with probably the most imaginative things flagged. Passing around a basket of grapes to share with an audience was deemed too risky in Manchester. Is this high level of fear across the entire spectrum of experience – from sexuality to the consumption of fruit – actually good for any of us?

Former chair of the U.K. Health and Safety Executive Dame Judith Hackitt, has this to say about the general question of risk:

> Overprotective parents and risk-averse teachers who do not enable children to learn to handle risk will lead to young adults who are poorly equipped to deal with the realities of the world around them, unable to discern real risk from trivia, not knowing who they can trust or believe.[58]

This overprotection goes both ways, too, with adults also deemed in need of safeguarding from the children. During one Mammalian project, a thirteen-year-old boy wanted to take a two-minute trip to a convenience store and, in this case, it was stated that it was *better he go alone* than be accompanied by an adult, as the concern was that the *adult* was vulnerable to the youth duplicitously fabricating a terrible fiction and ruining the adult's career. This in a neighbourhood famous for its violence – the reason the project was there in the first place! If he had been sent off alone to build his resilience, it would be one thing, but to protect the adult seems a bit much.

Social media is a constant headache for us, as our projects – like everybody else's – often utilize a variety of platforms to communicate with our audiences. In some situations, there are very strict rules about connecting online with the young people, with most such communication blocked by the institutions we work with. Even the mutual following that is the hallmark of public platforms like Instagram tends to be a no-no, presumably because that contact can lead to private conversations through direct messaging, and it is there people fear terrible things are going to happen. But, again, if everyone is brought together and briefed on what is cool and what is not, it would make these problems even less likely than they already are.

As it stands, the children are almost always completely unaware of a given organization's policy. No one bothers to tell them about the various prohibitions, so adults are forced to dance around the issue and act like weirdos trying to explain why a piggyback is a no-go. When a child excitedly runs at you to give you a hug, are you supposed to bend down and pretend to tie your shoe? While this might make sense for very young children who might be frightened by the implications of the policy, older kids and teenagers are aware that bad people exist, and would certainly be able to handle the knowledge, even if they, too, thought it a bit ridiculous.

Beyond complicating the immediate goals of a given project, the ban of online communication has implications for the long-term potential of any collaboration with young people. Once a project is finished, without the possibility of continued contact through the many channels available to us, the children evaporate from our lives. The Torontonians would not have happened had Sanjay not been able to easily contact me. It is no exaggeration to say that this method of working with youth owes its success entirely to online communication. Again, what operates here as a fail-safe against bad behaviour is openness, transparency, and responsibility to a wider community; the Torontonian Facebook group includes a lot of my adult collaborators and friends, so it contains a mix of people, and discussions are in the open, with a high degree of accountability.

Again the question can be asked: does the prohibition of online contact do more harm than good? Or are there some positives that get missed when intergenerational digital communication is prohibited? Does the potential for abuse warrant a prohibition against all electronic intergenerational contact within a pedagogical setting? Does prohibiting online contact between young people and the adults in a mentorship capacity – and I'll include teachers here – actually protect anyone from risk? It certainly starts to destabilize the idea of professional boundaries and a clear delineation between work and life. If you're suddenly online friends with a bunch of teen colleagues, you will be in their lives, if only just to glance at their family's dinner photos and catch a Snap of their dog taking a dump.

Related to this is a whole class of problems and challenges that stem from being a man working with children and the tedious suspicion that inevitably engenders. While women do not escape scrutiny, to be a middle-aged male working with children comes with the constant low-grade suspicion that you might be society's enemy number one. In America, the sealed-off areas between a school's unlocked doors and the locked doors monitored by staff are called 'man traps.'[59] This scrutiny is irksome but, unless you *are* a pedophile, it is just an occupational hazard: a slight carpal tunnel syndrome of the spirit – which can *really* hurt sometimes, but can be managed. In Mammalian's case, this is heightened because the work made with young people intentionally questions the power relationship between children and adults – not an especially comfortable line of inquiry given the amount of control that adults prefer to exert.

Touching is a sensitive subject in the U.K., in particular, with instructions always given to my team that fist-bumps and high-fives are as close as we are allowed to get to the children. A female collaborator got into trouble for piggybacking a girl whose feet were sore. In other places, like Germany, there is less worry, and hugging, as part of the greeting and farewell rituals, is entirely commonplace. The truth is that the prohibition against touch does nothing to protect children from people inclined to prey on them. If you're going to do something really, really bad to a child, some flimsy rule prohibiting all contact but a fist-bump or high-five is not going to get in your way.

For Mammalian, there hasn't been a problem, and the youth's friendship with some of the people they've met continues and has yielded other opportunities. This was easy to accomplish, since the people charged with leading the organization and protecting the youth were on the front line and constantly present. As the leaders of the organization, we were confident that the team was totally trustworthy. But Mammalian is tiny and, more often than not, the senior management of larger organizations can't be there to make sure all is okay.

Ultimately, there is no easy solution to this problem. Clear-headed assessments of the risk do little to relax people; low probabilities don't provide much solace if your child ends up being preyed upon, and the damaging effects are certainly not minimized by the fact that the chances were low. But it's crucial to examine situations as lucidly as possible and attempt to be clear on which situations put young people in danger, which are a case of unnecessary and irrational fear, and, worse, which situations are being policed to the detriment of children. In any case, the fact that there is a high level of concern that sometimes risks toppling into the ridiculous should not be surprising. In fact, artists working in this realm need to understand it as a necessary part of the gig, without which the artistic meaning would not be anywhere near as powerful or, for that matter, worth bothering with at all. It's because we're in the midst of this incredibly challenging situation that the work is so important.

Since the first wave of work with Parkdale Public School, we have emphasized networking and socializing. This second wave of the SMYLE focused on inducing deeper and more long-term collisions and collaborations between the youth and the artists who shared the youths' neighbourhood. This included both individual artists and the cultural and business institutions. We had four key institutional partners that contributed to the youths' growing social capital.

Evan Tyler's gallerywest was a venue for performances and longer-term programs and was, for a period, the location of our regular Friday Night Labs, an internal event with only the Torontonians where we engaged in several different activities, often using the space as an ad hoc studio for rehearsals, planning meetings, or just to chill on a Friday and watch horror films and *Family Guy*. We were honoured guests at all of Evan's openings, with the youth dropping by early to gaze at a bit of art and soak in the scene. The relationship with Evan is probably the most accurately in line with the call I made in *Social Acupuncture* for those with some personal resources to share and find ways to balance commercial or career objectives with social ones.

Another great example of such an entrepreneur is Christina Zeidler, who met the promise of her business's presence in the neighbourhood by providing us and the youth a subsidized office at her Gladstone Hotel – the kids were probably the world's first

Teenagers in Residence at a hotel. The hope was that they would naturally ladder into employment and, in fact, this has happened, with many of the youth doing casual gigs like coat check, and Nerupa Somasale landing a job as a marketing assistant.

Nerupa continued to tap the networks we shared when she was named Emerging Producer with the Luminato Festival, through a very competitive process, and is supervised by associate artistic director Naomi Campbell, the producer who put Mammalian on the map and co-developed *Haircuts by Children*. This is a great example of the SMYLE in action, as Nerupa and Naomi have known each other since Nerupa was fourteen, in a relationship that bordered on the familial. Sharing professional networks with the kids of Parkdale in a casual and ambient way was intended to fast-track the youth's acquisition of social and cultural capital; in this case, it clearly worked.

Through curator Mia Nielsen, the Drake Hotel provided us with a monthlong residency in one of its storefront spaces, where we housed our office and also an initiative called Grilled Open Cheese Office Songwriting Sandwich, offering the public songwriting workshops and a never-ending stream of grilled cheese sandwiches. The Theatre Centre launched their new building with a commitment to the youth through their presentation of *Promises to a Divided City,* a building-wide participatory funhouse intended to serve as a physical manifestation of the inequity in Toronto. Yan Wu at the Gendai Gallery was also generous with space, hosting a season of our Friday Night Labs, and, again, invited us to all the openings, where the youth chilled with art hipsters of all stripes.

These organizations and many other individuals culturally co-parented the youth, pitching in generously, giving us all kinds of opportunities and tiptoeing around our sprawling meetings, which took place pretty much everywhere, and enduring the noise while soaking up the fun that the youth would inevitably generate.

One of the aspects of the Torontonians that contributed to its success was something counterintuitive about working with young people: elitism. The team Sanjay and I assembled beginning in 2010 was a tight crew, many of whom had known each other since early childhood, with the understanding that current members had veto over new ones. Also counterintuitively, it was some of their closest friends whom they insisted on excluding, much to my irritation. They argued that it would reduce our collaboration into just another instance of school, where they were forced to associate in social configurations not of their choice or liking, or, for that matter, not ones that left them feeling safe and secure enough to take artistic or social risks. Further, although it was about creating a unique and safe environment for creative expression, there was also an element of elitism for elitism's sake that was absolutely crucial to the youth – they told me this clearly. They had a special thing going on and wanted to keep it as theirs and theirs alone, especially with respect to their closest friends – a tendency I'm sure most of us understand.

While this might seem like a glaring shortcoming of the model, it appears that way only because of the odd notion that youth engagement should be this open-access, egalitarian utopia, even though, for the most part, youth cultural consumption and participation is predicated on the same economic divisions and exclusions as the rest of the inequitable world. Youth arts programs directed at marginalized or other disadvantaged youth, however, are expected to somehow rise impeccably above these issues. This might, initially, seem entirely logical, particularly when we're talking about economic disadvantage, where programming is provided at no or low cost to youth who don't have easy access to cultural activities and training. But, as Bourdieu explains, art and culture are not and never have been neutral. He is clear on this point, noting this attribute of the sector is not just something contingent and off to the side, but central:

> The space of literary or artistic position-takings, i.e., the structured set of the manifestations of the social agents involved in the field – literary or artistic works, of course, but also political acts or pronouncements, manifestoes or polemics, etc. – is inseparable from the space of literary or artistic positions defined by possession of a determinate quantity of specific capital (recognition) and, at the same time, by occupation of a determinate position in the structure of the distribution of this specific capital.[60]

Which is to say, the arts are all about recognition, and recognition is not and cannot ever be distributed evenly. Of course not. Otherwise, fame would not even exist, and fame, even small-scale fame, is the purring engine of the entire industry; people want exceptional things, exceptional ideas, and exceptional experiences, and they want to attribute those to exceptional people. What is a great work of art if not, among other things, an exception?

To pretend this is not the current state of affairs and act in a utopian manner, believing in an impossible instantaneous equitable distribution where public programs targeted at marginalized youth are totally open to the participation of all, robs these programs of one of the most important values of cultural capital: the fact that everybody does not have it equally. While this position is no doubt anathema to a lot of people (including myself!) – especially people for whom engaging with youth and the arts is intended to *rectify* inequities and imbalances rather than exacerbate them – it is unfair to expect something like a youth arts program to address large-scale, systemic inequities. Those issues are important, but they have to be addressed at other levels through other means: progressive taxation; better approaches to determining, calculating, controlling, and distributing value; etc. These are big questions and not ones that artists can affect in any meaningful way – they're certainly not problems that a few piddly youth arts programs could ever hope to solve.

The case I put to the youth was that the likelihood of this small elite team of young people remaining around to run the company was extremely low. The goal is to train youths to assume control of the company; therefore, we always have to make sure we're working with a large enough pool of young people to ensure there's a chance that can happen.

They responded with this: 'We're cool to work with other youth, but they have to be from other neighbourhoods.'

Brilliant! Better than I could have ever hoped. They were thinking of geographic expansion, even as the motivation was to maintain their elite status locally. But in terms of a wider scale, they were cool to share the resources and good times we were having. I agreed without hesitation and we developed *How to Hook Up,* a yearlong exploration of other public youth arts programs in Toronto's suburbs, all in low-income neighbourhoods. This was followed by a year of AWKS, a series of awkward dance parties in the many fancy venues we worked in along Queen Street, which showcased the talents of the youth we had met from the suburbs.

To solidify our new relationship with these youth, we created *Promises to a Divided City*, a collectively created project using the new Theatre Centre as the lead character in a narrative about wealth, equity, and the city. *Promises to a Divided City* concluded the formal and programmatic training we engaged with the youth over the course of the four years of their high school (2010–2014). The first year was a period of cultural information gathering and tiny pilots, which continued to be a thread throughout the next three years of programs but which gradually took a back seat as the planning for *How to Hook Up*, AWKS, and *Promises to a Divided City* took precedence.

Creating social capital is easy: you just have to hang out with people and, ideally, enjoy their company. This key principle of the SMYLE is easily applied in sectors beyond arts and culture, where both formal and informal networking can easily incorporate young people who are being mentored. There will likely be some degree of awkwardness, but that's the price of building networks. Again, discomfort is absolutely central to this model and to the work of Mammalian in general, and should be embraced and not nervously avoided. The question of professionalism is also on the table yet again, with the youth likely to bring emotional and social dynamics to the party that many adults are keen to stamp out. When there's more of a familial vibe, people will have those annoying familial feelings, like love and hate.

This question is at the centre of what I'm proposing here and forms the SMYLE's revolutionary spine. In many sectors, but particularly those that include youth and other vulnerable populations, there is a strong professional adherence to very strict boundaries and a strong prohibition against breaching them with something as simple as friendship. In the case of work that is strictly targeted at healing, support, or advocacy, there may be a case for maintaining boundaries, but in situations where professional development, mentorship, and the creating of work come together – as is almost always the case with youth arts – these strict prohibitions against friendship are challenging impediments to effectively including young people in the industry. They disproportionately affect those youths whose parents are unfamiliar with the contours of the arts and culture sectors. This goes a long way toward explaining the industry's ongoing uniformity and homogeneity; cultural knowledge is passed from parent to child, so those whose parents are new to the country, or young people who are themselves newcomers, are at a distinct and intractable disadvantage with respect to local cultural forms. The entirety of the SMYLE is designed as a corrective to this as the sector takes a familial responsibility for the young people who live amongst us, embodying the proverb 'It takes a village to raise a child.' With the SMYLE, we pulled together a village of cultural uncles and aunts to welcome the young people into and familiarize them with the sector, to allow them to gain ambient knowledge by being surrounded by supportive adults who collaborate with and care for them. This brings us logically to the next SMYLE principle: friendship.

Friendship

A network is just a bunch of people shaking hands and spewing jargon, until friendships develop; thus social capital is followed logically by friendship. While this poses some questions around the protection of young people, it is doable with enough accountability and transparency, which require large numbers of co-mentors. As I mentioned above, I deliberately dragged the Torontonians to art openings, friends' parties, and parties at my own place, all very publicly, with the participation of prominent members of Toronto's cultural community, whom I invited into my world – they ended up learning as much as the kids, in a model of reciprocal mentorship.

The principle of friendship is probably the biggest challenge to implement in contexts other than the arts. Obviously, in many organizations, those leading the youth programming are in no position to invite the kids over to a party, making a public performance of the whole thing, as I did. But I believe that, within some contexts, there are ways to turn existing situations into opportunities to foster friendship. If taking the youth out to dinner is not possible, then maybe locating the places where there are similar opportunities to have conversations that are less formal and more personal is. Letty Clarke, from Aspex Gallery in Portsmouth, U.K., has found that the times she drives some of the youth home is a great opportunity to build trust. In fact, any sort of shared travel with the young people – whether public or private transport or even walking – is a great way to develop friendships.

This principle might seem impossible for a larger organization. However, in my assessment of the Art Gallery of Ontario, referred to earlier in this chapter, I found that many senior staff were open to building connections with those in the youth program. In small pilot events, the staff at the gallery demonstrated that they were interested in building social capital with the youth, and that, with someone responsible for logistical coordination, relationships could be built and maintained. For the pilot, this consisted of simple things like having a group of youth over for dinner, checking out a film together, and going skating. They were tiny events but still effective enough to begin to bridge the gap that exists between senior staff and the youth council. But, again, the speed of the organization – I actually saw staff members running down the halls from meeting to meeting – and the expediency with which things need to get done are strong impediments, leaving scant opportunity for the time it takes for real friendships to evolve without organized effort.

But to be friends with children and young people in this way tends to be dependent on modest numbers, which yield high impact, the next key principle.

Low Numbers, High Impact

Because friendship is an important component of this work, trust must be built slowly and organically; the next key principle is to start the youth engagement with very modest numbers and build things slowly, over time, organically, with other youth recruited through the efforts *of the youth themselves*. This supports the idea that we're serious about their full ownership of the organization, as they are making the calls about whom they collaborate with. As recognized by *Room to Rise*, the American study of four museums' youth programs, and corroborated by my own experience, as well as through discussions with others, this is a tough one for some funders to handle, because they want to see one of the few clearly quantifiable indicators: numbers, numbers, numbers. But what good is making little difference in many young people's lives?

In the case of Mammalian, it doesn't matter. We're not mandated to impact young people; we're mandated to make interesting art, and the young people we engage are not primarily conceived of as young people but, rather, our resident ensemble, our colleagues. Such a team is not helped by a revolving door of high numbers. Low numbers produce tightness and trust.

The way to better accept low numbers, beyond the immediate impact of healthy youth-to-adult ratios, is to realize that the work with the specific young people is only one site for considering the intervention and, in all likelihood, not even the most important. I also count a more broad neighbourhood or community effect to be a result of the work, where shifts of self-understanding might be triggered in those who are not involved but witness the activities of their peers, learning more about the general proclivities of the whole social group: if my friend can write and perform a song, certainly I can, too.

Additionally, the high impact of low numbers produces success to inspire other organizations in other places, which will, in turn, impact other youth. The sharing of the principles that produce the success of a modest intervention is an important site of the intervention itself, as news of the work spreads through panels, talks, and word of mouth, which relates to the principle of performativity – bringing actual things into being through the performance of them, the final key principle of the SMYLE.

Performativity

Performativity is a concept that is often mistaken for performance, but a performative act is more than just a performance. Originating in speech act theory, a performative act is more precisely one that brings things into being through the stating or performance of these things. The classic example is the statement 'I now pronounce you husband and wife' (or hubby/hubby, wife/wife, or whatever other gender-neutral variant you prefer). In that instant, a set of social relations are triggered that have major material implications for the lives of those just hitched. This work with youth brings real things into being. So, for example, *Haircuts by Children* isn't a performance *about* children's rights, because for the extent of the performance we give them the space to do what they want: we do our best to materialize these rights *for real*, even if only for the brief duration of an afternoon performance.

With the projects and other aspects of the work in Parkdale, the youth and I create unusual social circumstances in a public way. To do this, I drag them around the city and, now, around the globe, insisting they are at the table before anyone's sure what is actually on the table. This points back to the need for the work to be very public, particularly in the context of the more challenging principles, like social capital and friendship. We create a new and unusual social reality by performing that social reality, for the benefit of all in attendance and anyone who catches wind of what we're up to, something I deliberately amplify by talking and presenting about this work constantly, all around the world, often accompanied by the youth. This produces a public to which we are not only accountable but for whom we can provide inspiration.

Related to the idea of performativity is the effort we make to induce even the smallest of personal epistemic shifts within the young people – decisive shifts in their knowledge of themselves and their potential. Mostly these focus around abilities and capacities, with activities geared toward a scattershot approach, where we tirelessly expose the young people to a wide variety of ideas and events, even in the most casual way, with the conviction that the smallest of sparks can ignite a fire in people's understanding of their personal scope. These can even be the tiniest moments where a person does something they didn't think they could do. If we can make that idea stick, it can be applied across an entire life.

Additionally, a shift like that does not even necessarily have to happen to a person directly, but can be triggered by observing other individuals the person considers to be like them. So, for example, a young person might observe a close friend within her social circles write a song – an admittedly small act, but one that, if a person does not consider herself the 'kind' of person who can write songs, can have a major effect on self-understanding. Bourdieu is clear that one's habitus – our disposition and the embodiment of our cultural capital – is very difficult to transcend. It is tough to talk to a fish about air quality, in the same way that a person's self-concept may simply not encompass certain possibilities. It is not even that a person's self-conception includes the idea that 'I am not the kind of person who writes songs, makes films, invests in the stock market, etc.,' or that those capacities are not even included as things that a person is not; *they're simply excluded from any consideration at all.* Tossing people – particularly young people – into a variety of circumstances where they're asked to try a bunch of different activities, in a collegial collaboration with adults who are also forcing themselves to take risks and stretch their own capacities, is a reliable approach to chipping away at recalcitrant perceptions of the self and one's capacities. This is where lies the power of performativity, which might be broadly encapsulated in a succinct meme: *Fake it till you make it.*

Evaluating the SMYLE

What follows is a brief examination of the evaluation model I developed for the SMYLE, which looks at indicators and impacts that are different than the typical assessment of youth engagement, which focuses only on the youth. Here, because the goal is succession, the company and the individuals in it are an extra site of evaluation beyond the typical examination of impact on the youth; the latter is important but is often notoriously difficult to establish, with questions that only scratch the surface, and other indicators, like test scores, simply impossible to attribute to the intervention with anything resembling statistical confidence: there are simply too many confounding variables.

However, we can look to the stars for a useful metaphor. When astronomers gaze at distant galaxies, looking for celestial bodies, they often do not have the powers of magnification necessary to observe the planets that might be orbiting a star. However, they can observe the wobbling of the star as it responds to the gravitational influence of planets in its orbit. So too, with youth – we often cannot with any confidence attribute changes in their lives to our interventions. However, there is a larger, more visible body that can be observed with some level of accuracy: the organization delivering the programming, and the individuals who run it. These people can and should also be evaluated in terms of the effects the youth engagement is having on *them*. The focus on succession means we're on a two-way street – the adults in the organization should be learning as much from the youth as the youth are learning from them, even if that learning is simply how to better refine, develop, and expand the very activities the youth are engaged with: the youth program itself.

The youth, the organization, and the individuals in it who run the program can all be evaluated according to the different principles of the SMYLE. Below are a series of questions that can be asked with respect to the different stakeholders in the immediate sphere of the organization. It would not be difficult to consider other, more distant, stakeholders, like any businesses or other organizations that act as partners, and evaluate their participation in terms of the same principles and the effects of the work on them.

Succession

The youth: Are they getting paid? Are they learning how the company operates on all fronts? Do they have input? Are they affecting the direction of the company? Do they view themselves as working with the company in the future?

The company: Is the company paying the youth? Is it giving them meaningful responsibilities? Is it providing direction? Has the company changed because of the inclusion of youth?

The individuals in the company: Are we sharing our skills? Are we thinking about evolving our role in the company to make room for incoming youth?

Collegiality

The youth: Do the youth feel the work matters to both parties? Is there shared ownership? Do they consider the company partly theirs?

The company: Is work with youth as important as other aspects of the company? Does it occupy the 'mainstage'? Are youth involved in day-to-day decisions? Are they involved in long-term visioning?

The individuals in the company: Do we feel the work with the youth is central to the company? Do we feel the youth are colleagues on par with other established professionals? Does the work matter to us as artists? Does it have a measurable effect on our careers?

Division of Labour

The youth: Are the young people contributing content through their natural impulses and interests? Is the content based on activities that would not ordinarily be considered 'programming'?

The company: Are we providing the time for the young people and adults to collaborate in an easy manner, where people are simply themselves? Have the adults in the company established themselves as experts in particular forms? Are we working with great professional artists, or are these people for whom working with children is a reluctant Plan B?

The individuals in the company: Do we know the youth well enough to design projects around their interests?

Social Capital

The youth: Can the youth use these friendships as references, to learn more about what's happening in the city, for opportunities to participate, for learning and earning?

The company: Are we sharing our networks effectively? Do our networks understand what we are doing with succession? Is the benefit mutual?

The individuals in the company: Are we sharing their personal networks with the youth? Are these networks providing opportunities for learning and earning? Is the benefit mutual?

Friendship

The youth: Do the young people have different friends than they would have had they not worked with the company? And, in particular, adults in the culture industries?

The company: Does time spent between company members and youth extend past the bounds of the working relationship? Does a company soirée look different than before the succession plan?

The individuals in the company: Are friendships developing outside the bounds of the work? How deep are those friendships?

Myself: Have my friendships been affected by the youth? Do I have friendships with the young people?

Low Numbers/High Impact

The youth: Is it a small, tight group of young people who all identify strongly as members of the company? Do they display a strong sense of ownership bordering on possessiveness? Do they want to exert control and veto over recruitment?

The company: Can the company make a good case for low numbers to the funders?

The individuals in the company: Do we have a good knowledge of who the young people are? Is the ratio of youth to adult a productive one?

Performativity

The youth: Does the work position the youth centrally and in a position of power? Is any work with the youth *about* their power, or does it actually give space for their assumption of power?

The company: Does the company promote the work with the youth among the most important things they're doing? Is the presence of the youth changing the organization in a meaningful way?

The individuals in the company: Is the presence of the youth changing our lives?

The SMYLE's evaluative model is a conceptual comb to pass through a situation and see where improvements can be made, knowing that there will be snags and adjustments and that the model is flexible enough to be applied in more formal situations than Mammalian, where just the asking of many of the questions has the potential to trigger different ways of considering things.

While I have not presented the work chronologically, each year did build logically on the previous one, beginning with a year of primarily socializing and small projects to get to an understanding of the arts and culture scene in Toronto (2010–2011); a year of learning the rudiments of event production through the *Producers of Parkdale* (2011–2012); a year of getting to know the youth in other areas of the city through *How to Hook Up* (2012–2013); and a year of presenting the work of these other youth in parties along Queen Street West in *AWKS* (2013–2014); and culminating in a theatre-based immersive performance, *Promises to a Divided City* (2014), that brought together all the youth in a discussion of inequity in the city.

The logical coherence in the way the programming unfolded was not the result of strategic planning but, as I've mentioned, simply a response to the needs and desires of the young people themselves. Ideas and structure emerged unpredictably but logically as a natural result of the needs, desires, and demands of the youth, which would be channelled and turned to our advantage in ways we could not have foreseen. For example, the elitism that saw the youth refusing to allow their nearby peers to participate triggered a kind of compromise – the connection with youth from Toronto's inner suburbs – which had none of the qualities of a typical compromise. In fact, it pushed all of us further, built our networks, and yielded creative connections that continue to this day, with Feroz Syed, one of the youth who joined because of these efforts, currently part of the regular team that directs *Nightwalks with Teenagers* internationally.

The effects of the presence of these particular young people have had important and lasting impact on Mammalian and myself, so much so that it's impossible to plan for the future without constant consultation and collaboration with them. They are on the board of directors, work as staff, and are among the consistent set of collaborators who we work with on projects both in Toronto and, on the road, internationally. Another goal beyond succession has been to replicate the model in other places, with other organizations and other youth. At this time, there are two areas in which the ideas are being applied: in Germany with the Ruhrtriennale Festival, and in London with the London International Festival of Theatre.

The Ruhrgebiet is a post-industrial urban area with a number of cities acting as centres within the agglomeration, including Essen, Bochum, Duisburg, Dortmund, and Gelsenkirchen. The population is spread out, which makes working with youth especially challenging, since they tend to be limited in terms of quick and easy mobility. But even though the population is spread out, so are the activities of the Ruhrtriennale, a large-scale seven-week-long performing arts festival.

Mit Ohne Alles is a collective of young people that was spun out of the *Children's Choice Awards*, which we ran at the Ruhrtriennale Festival for three years (2012–2014). Our 2015 project, *Millionen, Millionen, Millionen*, was a stage-based presentation in response to the original youths' desire to work with less advantaged youth, where we brought in about thirty recent arrivals to the country, hailing from Syria, Gambia, Albania, Afghanistan, Portugal, and Holland. In August 2016, eleven of the Toronto youth went to Germany to participate in a three-week intensive mentorship, sharing training and skills with the German youth. Teentalitarianism is an umbrella project, a mini-festival within the festival, focused on work created by teenagers, as the young people took over Atelier Van Leishout's massive festival installation *The Good, the Bad and the Ugly*, basically reproducing what we did along Queen Street in Toronto over the course of five years, but within the seven-week blitz of the festival.

Festival dramaturge Cathrin Rose has embraced and contributed to the development of the SMYLE's principles, with the project clearly breaching work/life balance by including her daughter, Emma. Cathrin goes to great lengths to maintain the participation of the young people, and has developed meaningful relationships with the youth and their families.

The Tottenham UpLIFTers is a six-year (2015–2020), multi-project creative learning program delivered by the London International Festival of Theatre (LIFT) in collaboration with two schools in the London neighbourhood of Tottenham that share a building: Northumberland Park School and the Vale, the latter working with physically and developmentally disabled students. We are targeting a single-grade cohort of thirty Northumberland Park and five Vale students, working with them for their entire school career, until 2020, with exactly the same long-term intention: succession, to bring any of the young people who are interested into both LIFT and the Mammalian community of collaborators, including the

Torontonians, Mit Ohne Alles, the Ruhrtriennale, and any other interested organizations.

In 2011, Tottenham was the site of riots that quickly spread through social media to cities all over the country. High youth unemployment and rising inequity in the area have created a situation where people feel they have no stake in society, and without a stake, there's little reason to contribute and every reason to push against these circumstances. Additionally, Tottenham has been identified in the 2011 London Plan as both an Opportunity and an Intensification area. Opportunity areas are the city's major reservoir of brownfield land with significant capacity to accommodate new housing and commercial and other development linked to existing or potential improvements to public transport accessibility. Between now and 2025, there is the hope that an additional 5,000 jobs will be created in the community, as well as 10,000 new homes. Which pretty much means one thing: gentrification is coming to Tottenham. In fact, it's already there if you look carefully enough, with the hallmark disused industrial spaces filled with bustling artists, targeted condominium development that manages to be almost a gated community of its own, and a slight shift in local businesses as they prepare for the rapid descent of a new clientele. The children and I recently observed a pod of cultural workers ensconced in an espresso café, happy and warm in their natural habitat, all mesmerized by their laptops.

We are at a moment that is similar to what was experienced on a very small scale in Toronto with the gentrification of West Queen West, and the Tottenham UpLIFTers project is intended to get a jump on the process, to develop a team of young people who will be in great shape to respond to the changes. Hopefully the project will help the youth be resilient against displacement pressures and also feel party to the party – participating in the changes, with an informed understanding of the social processes and with allies among some of the others, like artists, who will also face rising rents and coffee prices, as well as some of the new businesses and other institutions that are inevitably on their way.

The program's start replicates some of the first years in Parkdale, bringing artists into the school to meet and work with the children;

year two features public interventions out in the real world, with the children at centre stage, but this time with the local artists as leads, pitching their idea to the children to see what they produce, together. Years three, four, and five replicate the three years of the Torontonians that included socializing and meeting the cultural community, immersion into the logistics of event production, and, finally, the development of a project to be presented at LIFT in 2020. It's a balance between needing a clear path to secure the support and buy-in of the school and funders, and permitting enough flexibility for surprising things to emerge and be followed, without knocking the whole thing off the rails.

With Mit Ohne Alles and the UpLIFTers, we are seeing evidence of the sorts of connections and caring the model was designed to trigger. With respect to the overall project's big prize – the inclusion of the young people not only into the sector, but into the organizations running the programs – it's clear that there is a high level of commitment to the idea, and that things are being put in place to support this. This is a straightforward result of facilitating the various principles of the SMYLE: when friendships occur, caring follows, and with caring comes a commitment to the long term.

5

CHILDREN VS. THE FUTURE

Following the lead of children and making space for the kids to participate in all matters affecting them, thereby increasing their role in shaping our future, will not be so easy. We're living in strange and contradictory times in this adultitarian world of ours. In many ways, life has never been better for the kids. After thousands of years of being bossed around by parents, teachers, priests, police, and other authority figures,[61] the last decades have brought about rapid changes, with the United Nations Declaration of Human Rights (1948) and the Convention on the Rights of the Child (1989) ushering in new attitudes in many parts of the world. The result is that, among others things, spanking is now illegal in forty-three countries, and growing;[62] most teachers are banned from the strap; many children are spared the most horrible forms of labour; and their views are considered by courts in situations like custody disputes.

Over the course of the twentieth century, children have evolved from beings who were barely, if at all, considered legitimate humans, to a class of people who, now, suffer quite the opposite problem: they are considered all too human, entirely vulnerable to every conceivable exploitation and violence. Psychologist and linguist Steven Pinker, in his survey of the global decline of violence, notes this precipitous drop in aggression toward children and the commensurate increase in their value, using a memorable phrase: 'The historical increase in the valuation of children has entered its decadent phase.'[63]

Evidence of this decadence is abundant, as the protection of children has reached mind-blowing levels of absurdity. Even as violence across the entire spectrum has dropped, children's ability to explore the world on their own has been, for all intents and purposes, outlawed;[64] parents have been investigated for allowing their children to play unattended in their own backyard;[65] grass has been deemed too hard a surface for playgrounds;[66] teens are being charged for exploiting themselves by texting photos that are, at best, slightly seductive, but not revealing, let alone licentious;[67] and the DVD release of the first years of the groundbreaking children's television show *Sesame Street* comes with the warning 'These early *Sesame Street* episodes are intended for grownups, and may not suit the needs of today's preschool child.'[68]

These are just a few examples of the insanity out there, all relentlessly documented by America's Worst Mother, Lenore Skenazy, on her harrowing blog, Free Range Kids (freerangekids.com), which oscillates from being utterly depressing to uproariously hilarious – sometimes simultaneously. Combing through Skenazy's abundant examples, it is hard not to agree with Pinker that things have totally toppled over into a ridiculous decadence that cannot be good for the kids. Indeed, Pinker provides a horrifying statistic that sums up the situation nicely: 'More than twice as many children are hit by cars driven by parents taking their children to school as by other kinds of traffic.'[69] This ironic, unintended consequence of the irrational fear of allowing children to walk to school is mirrored in other statistics focused on child obesity and the growing incidence of mental illness. As things have gotten safer in the world; as international treaties and national laws have intervened and recognized the rights of children; as children have been folded into the market as powerful consumers and trendsetters; as the internet has positioned the kids as competent agents, not only the subjects of interesting social developments in the world, but driving them – why has this period of safety, increasing rights, and growing influence also produced the current moral panic that keeps young people swaddled, coddled, and cloistered well into their adults years?

Perhaps this is not a contradiction at all but a causal relationship. As the rights of children have rocketed up the agenda in the decades following World War II, this moral panic and obsession with health and safety during the struggle to redefine the role of children is simply evidence of a phase shift: turbulence is to be expected as adults push back against the erosion of their influence. The fact is that the family, parents, school system, and State are losing – and must lose – the monopoly of control they've exerted for years: the children are no longer their property, but rights holders, like anyone else. The implications of this have not been fully defined or understood and, in the meantime, this new legitimacy of children has left many stakeholders simply trying to cover all bases, ultimately seeking to do what they imagine is best for the children, but invoking extreme visions of danger and enacting bizarre overcompensation in the process. I see this all the time when working with schools that, acting *in loco parentis*, are far more restrictive of freedom than most parents. They cannot afford to make even a tiny mistake while they uphold a level of protection that is at least as strict as the most overprotective, paranoid, and oppressive parent, lest they incur litigious wrath. School administrators can only be as lenient and trusting as the least lenient and trusting parent. So, too, other stakeholders, particularly the State, in their various duties to the child, are forced to always consider the worst-case scenario, even when that leads to irrational behaviour that harms more children than it protects. In response to the rising rights of children, their growing power and influence, there's a society-wide panic that can legitimately be expressed only in concerns about the children's safety, as crazy as some of those concerns are. And, as crazy as they are, they all demonstrate the adults' ultimate desire for control and dominance over children.

Hopefully this overreach will have a brief tenure, and a correction is imminent, as we reach the nadir of this decadence and people begin to critically assess the situation, take a rigorous look at the data, and finally come to terms with the fact that children have never been safer, pushing the pendulum back toward a more rational view that accepts that children are, finally, people with the same rights as everyone else and not, as they are now in practice, the last visible minority still subject to legally permitted discrimination.

As this fleeting historic blip that pulled the children away from the labour market toward a precious pricelessness concludes, we have a responsibility to make sure their reintegration into the market happens ethically and for their benefit, where they have some control over the value they produce. This is going to be particularly challenging, as the twenty-first century is likely to see historically unprecedented inequity,[70] the brunt of which, like all social inequity, will be borne by children. This skyrocketing inequity is what makes this proposal all the more urgent, since children, with their obsession with justice, are some of the staunchest advocates of fairness, even as this dedication is often framed as the unrealistic idealism of youth. But considering the horrifying historic lack of success with so-called realistic solutions to social inequity, maybe it is time for something a little nutbar. This is where the embarrassed revolutionary, in sheer desperation, gets over his embarrassment for naively hoping the world can be a more fair place and starts to cast around for innovative solutions to the structural and always increasing inequity that is the hallmark of capitalism.

I'm calling on the arts and culture, in particular, to pilot this scheme, because of a property unique to these realms, something no others possess, a near-magical quality: the permission to pretend. This permission, to create and tell stories, is both a unique power and something that, again, children are expert at. The power to pretend is much more than simple mimicry; it is the power of performativity, where art functions as a magical shroud or cloak, allowing us to get away with things – like children styling hair – that are not only well outside permissible norms, but manage to bring impossibilities into momentary existence to prove they can actually happen.

In the most recent round of the fight to change the world, art and culture were pummelled to a pulp, distracted by an indulgent Warholian delusional decadence that found beauty in the drug-addled destitution of late modernity, where mental illness was an indicator of coolness and a detached urbanity pretended to be too hip for the system, as the system scooped up these supposed anti-authoritarian individuals and brought them easily back into the world of corporate authority, like lost Alzheimer's patients gently guided by the elbow back into the padded comfort of the psych ward, still under the delusion that they own their individuality. Artists abandoned a vision of an equitable humanity in exchange for their photo on the cover of the entertainment weekly, that antiquated communication technology that has all but vanished, as Warhol's fifteen minutes of fame has become a temporal Möbius strip we're all living over and over again as we marvel at the wit of our own status updates, keeping careful count of the thumbs-ups appearing as real-time notifications on our phones.

It is time for art and culture to vindicate itself, making good on the promises of a pre-Warholian desire to infuse life with art and chip away at the monopoly that capitalism holds over our imaginations, rediscovering the unfulfilled Beuysian promise that understands the aesthetic as not all about style but as an antidote to the anaesthetic, Warhol's droll and arrogant numbness that artsters continue to propagate as they still insist – some fifty years after the fact – on posing for selfies with the inert death mask of the man himself.[71] You don't often see children affecting detachment, because children regard detachment as bullshit, and they will quickly call you on that crap. Instead of being cool, the arts need to start warming things up, healing the rifts that are threatening to rip the social fabric into a multitude of tiny ribbons, and accepting that things are going to get a lot more uncomfortable before we can ever be comfy again.

In April 2016, when the U.K.'s performance community gathered at the Tate Modern for the Live Art Development Agency's symposium surrounding Sybille Peters's performance art game for families, *Playing Up*, this crowd of practitioners who had been raised on a diet of edgy work that pushed boundaries around gender, sexuality, and the body agreed that such transgressive performances of yesteryear look downright quaint and have done little to jam the gears of capital. There was a consensus that those wanting to take artistic risk these days need look no further than the kids, whose very bodies are sites of pitched and bloody ideological battles, lightning rods for moral panic, and incessant lobbyists for the concept of fairness. Say what you will about the risk that performance artist Chris Burden took with his seminal work *Shoot*, in which he was shot in the arm with a .22 rifle, no one was going to wonder if he was society's enemy number one: a pedophile. There are very real risks and monumental challenges that come bundled with even the most benign of artistic collaborations with children, where a piggyback is likely to get you called down to the head teacher's office for a stern reprimand, if not booted out of the school entirely.

Through working with children in the arts to create performative realities that bring Bourriaud's microtopias into reality, even for mere moments, where the universal subject is the vulnerable subject and the idea of fairness utterly logical, we can begin to test and model new ways of being together. Once we've got a handle on how this can transpire in creative settings – without harming a hair on anyone's head – we can share our insights with the rest of world, parachuting kids into all walks of life: little guerrillas whose strategic skill is simply their incapacity to tolerate the cruel expediency and gruelling demands of a world of work that floods all areas of life, where even the most leisurely moments are assiduously documented, treated with filters, and cast into the world to prove that we still matter. Children's demand for play and their intolerance of boredom are incredibly powerful skills that can and should be mobilized against a coercive capitalist professionalism intent on sanitizing the world of anything but the most bland utterance, where even an expression of love – *especially* an expression of love – is a radical, risky, and revolutionary act.

APPENDIX 1

THE PERFORMANCE WORK OF MAMMALIAN DIVING REFLEX AND DARREN O'DONNELL IN COLLABORATION WITH CHILDREN AND YOUNG PEOPLE[72]

Works with Children in Parkdale, 2005–2009

2005
Diplomatic Immunities: Life at Age Nine

Diplomatic Immunities: Life at Age Nine was part of a series of performances that featured a team of artists travelling around a variety of sites, focusing on various themes, talking to people in public, and using performances to report on what we found. For *Life at Age Nine*, the team met a class of fourth graders from Parkdale Public School, had a chat with them, then discussed these chats with an audience at Toronto's Buddies in Bad Times Theatre.

2006
Haircuts by Children

Haircuts by Children, which is exactly how it sounds, was created in collaboration with the same class of fourth graders as *Diplomatic Immunities: Life at Age Nine* and was presented on four weekends in May, each hair salon at a different point of the compass. Since 2006, *Haircuts by Children* has been presented in thirty-seven cities around the world, and counting. It is a whimsical relational performance that playfully engages with the enfranchisement of children, trust in the younger generation, and the thrills and chills of vanity. *Haircuts by Children* involves children from the ages of eight to twelve who are trained by professional hairstylists, then paid to run a real hair salon, offering members of the public free haircuts. It has been performed in Austin, Birmingham, Bologna, Calgary, Copenhagen, Cork, Darwin, Derry, Dublin, Enschede, Ghent, Glasgow, Hull (U.K.), Kuopio, Launceston, Los Angeles, London, Melbourne, Milan, Montreal, Newcastle, New York City, Norwich, Nyon, Perth, Portland, Prague, Regina, Sydney, Terni, Tokyo, Toronto, Trondheim, Vancouver, Victoria, Vienna, Whitehorse, and Winchester.

Ballroom Dancing

Ballroom Dancing was an all-ages dance party held at Toronto's inaugural Nuit Blanche, featuring many of the same students who worked on *Haircuts by Children* and *Life at Age Nine*. *Ballroom Dancing* brought adults and children together to dance to tunes selected and controlled by the kids, who DJed in a gymnasium filled with more than 2,700 rubber balls. A safe playtime was fostered to counter the prevailing view that the public sphere is a place of danger, atomization, and awkwardness rather than safety, communication, and styling moves. Later in the evening, after the kids had gone to bed, the safe playtime was usurped by the adults, who insisted on a massive game of murderball where they managed to generate ten eye injuries, several broken glasses, a fat lip, a dislocated knee, and a broken scaphoid – the most litigated bone in the body.

2007–2008

Parkdale Public School vs. Queen Street West

Parkdale Public School vs. Queen Street West was a yearlong collaboration with Parkdale Public School that brought together the children of Parkdale and the various cultural institutions, businesses, and art hipsters along Queen Street West, just as the gentrification of the neighbourhood was starting to hit its stride. *Parkdale Public School vs. Queen Street West* featured ten different performance projects over the course of the 2007–2008 school year:

- *The Children's Choice Awards* was an intervention into Alley Jaunt, an annual art exhibition that featured work in people's garages in the area surrounding Trinity Bellwoods Park. A group of Parkdale Public School students looked at all the work and awarded their favourites with chocolate-coated trophies. *The Children's Choice Awards* continues to be produced internationally and is now more specifically conceived of as an intervention into the structure and institution of an arts festival, where a group of ten-year-olds from local public schools is appointed the official festival jury, chauffeured to and from festival shows to see the art, take notes, and size it all up. The jury responds to criteria they have created from their vast expertise, and collectively they determine award categories and vote on the winners. The project culminates in a ceremony where the kids present handmade trophies to the winners, all decided by them, and described in their own words. *The Children's Choice Awards* has so far been presented in Brussels, Edinburgh, Kitchener, Kuopio, Kyoto, London, Melbourne, Norwich, Oldenburg, Perth, the Ruhrgebiet, Toronto, and Vancouver. An ongoing blog dedicated to the project exists at childrenschoiceawards.blogspot.ca/.

- *The Children's Choice Dinner* was a special event held in conjunction with the inaugural *Children's Choice Awards*. The young jury members invited their favourite artist from Alley Jaunt as their guest to a dinner at Coca Tapas and Wine Bar, generously provided by chef Nathan Isberg.

- *The Beautiful Hungry City* was a five-installment dinner-and-speaker series, each featuring two speakers whose vocation fortifies civil society but is not normally associated with beauty. It was sponsored by the City of Toronto's Live with Culture office and occurred at a variety of restaurants in Parkdale and nearby areas. The kids from Parkdale Public School were invited and brought their parents and little brothers and sisters. They got bored, ran around, listened, learned, and met all of the speakers. The speakers included Armand Cousineau, a data analyst and project coordinator working on campaign strategies for not-for-profits and charitable organizations; Marney Isaac, an ethnobiologist studying soil and the impact of crop rotation as it relates to urban geography; firefighter and dancer Stacey Hannah; Steve Comilang, a Tagalog court interpreter; Ed Lau, the owner of the Common café; Mai Ly, a physiotherapist; Sarah Mackie, a flight attendant; Yvonne Ng, a film archivist; and Mike Street and Shiraz Vally, both paramedics.

- *Shortcuts and Hangouts* was presented in association with Jane's Walk and featured urban geography from the perspective and authority of the kids. The Grade 8 geography students gave an animated walking tour of Parkdale, showing a public audience their secret hangouts and shortcuts, and sharing their thoughts on the best and worst their neighbourhood has to offer, and what could make it better.

- *Walk the Block* consisted of a series of encounters between the younger kids at the Parkdale Public School, an artist, and the neighbourhood. Seven of Toronto's most interesting artists took the kids out on a spin around the block and engaged them in an artistic gesture. Diane Borsato led Ms. Wurtz's Grade 1s in an unlikely morning of milkshakes and mushrooms, taking the students to a nearby Indian restaurant for mango lassis, and then back to the school to watch a short lecture on fungus. Diane elaborated on the most colourful, repulsive-smelling, oddly shaped, and surprisingly named mycological fruitings, and the students assigned their own names to the mushrooms and choreographed dances for the fungi. Ulysses Castellanos took Ms. Morris's Grade 2 students to Dollarama, where they bought a pile of toys, took them back to the school, and broke them into a million fragments. Then they made new toys. Zanette Singh took Ms. Seto's Grade 1 students outside to scour the neighbourhood for materials to create doll creatures. The children then found special secret locations around the area to install their creations. Hannah Miami invited Ms. Adam's Grade 2 students to harvest an entire field of dandelions, then beautifully arrange them throughout a park, leaving an organic sculpture for others to discover. Swintak introduced the idea of 'urban quicksand' to Ms. Serpa's Grade 1s, who discussed their knowledge of quicksand and drafted a Top 10 list of places in Toronto where they would like to see quicksand pits. The kids assembled their own miniature quicksand-pit kits, took them outside, and placed them around the neighbourhood. Mr. Montenaro's Grade 3 students worked with Stephanie Comilang to create messages of love, which were then posted around the neighbourhood. Sandy Plotnikoff took Ms. Wong's Grade 3 students thrift-shopping at local Parkdale stores. They then made quick, fun alterations to their purchases.

- *At the Kids' Table* was created in collaboration with Nathan Isberg and Coca Tapas and Wine Bar and featured a student-designed prix-fixe menu. The students ran Coca for the evening, hosting, serving, cooking, plating, and eating their delicious creations. The restaurant was open to the audience to enjoy the dinner/performance by the young chefs.
- *The Parkdale Strings vs. Blocks Recording Club* featured the senior strings band, under the direction of Mr. Curry, who collaborated with local hipster indie-record label Blocks Recording Club and the bands Kids on TV, the Phonemes, and Bob Wiseman. Together with the students, they participated in musical workshops that culminated in a public performance at the Gladstone Hotel.
- *The ADD DJs vs. LAL* featured the participation of Rosina Kazi and Nicholas Murray of the band LAL, who trained the children in the art of DJing. The students spun their stuff and performed at the Gladstone Hotel, during *The Parkdale Strings vs. Blocks Recording Club.*
- *Parkdale Art Students vs. Mercer Union* featured the students' thoughts and perspectives on *Thank you, come again! / Obrigado, volte sempre!*

/ *Merci, revenez bientôt!*, a show at Mercer Union Centre for Contemporary Art that brought together Brazilian artist Ana Teixeira and Toronto-based artist Anne Fauteux in a two-month residency and exhibition. In response to the social-practice-based works of the artists, the students also created their own street performance, *Crush-4-Crush* and *Flower-4-a-Scar*.

- *Show and Tell*, co-directed by Stephanie Comilang and me, is a feature-length video portrait of every one of the 647 students at Parkdale Public School in May 2008 and presents their favourite things: Transformers, basketballs, Tweety Bird, and erasers.

2009
Eat the Street

Eat the Street, first created in collaboration with the students of Parkdale Public School, is a sister project to *The Children's Choice Awards* and, like the latter project, continues to tour today. It features a group of young people who, over roughly two weeks, make stops at several of a city's most notable eateries, where they are dined, though not wined. In the first iteration, the restaurants were all located along Queen Street West, the kids' own neighbourhood.

The children are feted, fed, and charged with offering their brutally honest, uncensored opinions on the food, the service, the decor, the state of the washrooms, and the charm of the servers. For the cost of a meal, the public is invited to sit among the kids for a front-row view of the youthful connoisseurs in action. The project concludes with an award ceremony, where the restaurants are celebrated for, among other things, having the 'Coolest Chef' and the 'Scariest Washroom.' *Eat the Street* has been presented in Birmingham, Cagliari, Cork, Launceston, Regina, Terni, Toronto, and Vancouver. An ongoing blog dedicated to the project can be found at eatdastreet.blogspot.ca.

Works with the Torontonians/Young Mammals, 2010–2017

The Torontonians were an intergenerational art collective triggered by then-fourteen-year-old Sanjay Ratnan that, between the years 2010 and 2017, created a body of work in Toronto and internationally. The collective has evolved and expanded into the Young Mammals, a wing of Mammalian Diving Reflex dedicated to training and succession.

2010

- *How to Be a Brown Teen* is a video starring Sanjay Ratnan in the role of a strict headmaster who instructs his students – Ahash Jeeva and Nerupa Somasale – on the fine art of being a South Asian teenager living in the West.
- *Networking 101* was a performance created for the Art Gallery of York University's Performance Bus, which took the public from downtown Toronto on the forty-five-minute bus ride to the North York gallery. The performance featured the Torontonians meeting members of the public and vetting them for future collaborations. The performance produced a long-term collaborative relationship with cellist Anupa Khemadasa Perera, who continues to work with some of the young people.
- *You, Too, Can Be 14* was a performance created for Treehouse Talks and featured the Torontonians teaching adults how to be fourteen again. Instruction included: breakdancing, dancing to Michael Jackson's *Thriller*, how to slap a bald guy, how to jump over a table, and math.

2011–2012

- *Farmer's Market 2050* was presented by the Justina M. Barnicke Gallery as part of the 2011 Nuit Blanche, at the University of Toronto's Hart House Quad. The project anticipated that in 2050 the world's population would exceed nine billion people, resulting in extreme food shortages. It featured the ideas of architect Kubo Dzamba and his concept of Third Millennium Farming – the raising of crickets on algae grown on the city's grey water – and chef Nathan Isberg's culinary treatment of the insects, with the teens offering scientific interpretation of the event.
- *Nightwalks with Teenagers* is a walking performance created in collaboration with the Torontonians that continues to tour internationally. The project features two groups of young people – one local and the other from the original Toronto team – who plan, design, and lead public walks through the city at night, exploring areas that are new to both the youth and their adult audience. *Nightwalks with Teenagers* is focused on the pro-social ameliorative power of walking together, and is inspired in part by the Situationist notion of the 'derive,' as well as psychogeographic wanderings through the city. It has been performed in Basel, Bochum, Bristol, Duisburg, Hamilton,

Inverness, Leeds, Manchester, Newcastle, Nuuk, Nyon, Riga, and Saint-Étienne.

- *Dare Night*, conceived by then-fifteen-year-old Nerupa Somasale, is part performance, part party game. Audience members are put to the test by executing a series of hilarious, exhilarating, and shocking dares all designed by a team of teenagers, who are sometimes known to slip in planted dares to showcase their own performance skills. *Dare Night* has been presented in Bochum, Reykjavik, and Toronto.
- *Grilled Open Cheese Office Songwriting Sandwich*, a residency at the Gladstone Hotel where Mammalian opened our office to the public, keeping typical hours of operations, was focused on a month of songwriting workshops with the Torontonians and a culminating performance of *Dare Night*.
- *The Producers of Parkdale* was a yearlong mentorship residency at the Gladstone Hotel where ten teens learned the ropes of event production: curating, budgeting, marketing, production management, and hospitality. The mentorship was a three-pronged process, with workshops, shadowing, and office/event production. The teens were mentored in arts management and production from top culture makers in Toronto, including Naomi Campbell, Yan Wu, Chris Lorway, Carrie Sager, Howard Mah, Nathan Isberg, Sarah Robayo Sheridan, Julian Sleath, Mathew Kensett, and Lisa Duke, as well as Gladstone staffers led by Britt Welter-Nolan and Noa Bronstein. The youth curated and managed an all-night happening, *Dare Night: Lockdown*, a public sleepover/event-filled *Dare Night* in the Gladstone Hotel's ballroom. In anticipation of the event, they ran a full-time office at the Gladstone to prepare, spending their summer holidays publicizing, budgeting, and creating schedules.
- *Friday Night Labs* was a regular Friday-night meet-up at Gendai Gallery to work on projects.

2012–2013

- *How to Hook Up* was a yearlong research and short documentary series created by the Torontonians that focused on the young people who participate in some of Toronto's other youth arts programs, including Just BGRAPHIC, Arts for Children and Youth, Art Starts, and Urban Arts.
- *Sleeping with Family*, conceived by me and co-directed with Nicole Bazuin, is a short documentary about sleeping arrangements in a

low-income neighbourhood, as described by fifteen teenagers living in Parkdale. Disguised to protect their identities, the young people in the film discuss their living conditions, particularly the absence of – and negotiations for – privacy, as they live in close quarters with multiple family members.

- *Allegations: A Re-enactment of the Mayor Rob Ford Crack Video*, conceived by Virginia Antonipillai and directed by me, was a restaging of the video of Toronto's infamous mayor Rob Ford smoking crack, complete with a behind-the-scenes interview with the teens who made the video.

- *Teenagers in Residence* (2012–2015) saw youth assume residencies in the Gladstone Hotel, where Mammalian was generously provided subsidized office space. Beyond the many projects we created while in residency, a number of the young people made a bit of extra cash working the coat check, and Torontonian Nerupa Somasale was employed in the Gladstone office as marketing assistant.

- *Friday Night Labs* was a regular Friday night meet-up at Evan Tyler's gallerywest to work on current projects.

2013–2014

- *AWKS*, conceived by Tenzin Chozin and Ngawang Luding, was a series of awkward dance parties at venues along Queen Street, including gallerywest, the Theatre Centre, the Great Hall, the Ground Level Cafe and the Gladstone Hotel. *AWKS* was designed to showcase the youth who the Torontonians/Young Mammals had met during the previous year's *How to Hook Up*.

- *Get Out of My Room*, conceived by the Torontonians, was presented as part of the Gladstone Hotel's annual alternative design event, Come Up to My Room. The youth created a hyper-teen bedroom complete with dirty laundry, piles of neglected homework, and clusters of real live young people transfixed by video games.

- *Promises to a Divided City*, presented by the Theatre Centre, was a massive multi-roomed participatory performance starring the Torontonians and other GTA youth who presented data about the city's growing inequity and the effects inequity has on the physical body. Taking as a starting point the ideas of Andrew Carnegie – the benefactor who donated the money to create the library that now houses the Theatre Centre – particularly his dictum that 'those who die wealthy die disgraced,' *Promises to a Divided City* explored the civic responsibility of the affluent. The show had a cast of over thirty teen performers, and blasted the audience through economic and biological realities, landing them into a cosy utopian vision of what Toronto has to offer if given leadership with a modicum of vision.

- *High School Health*, directed by Nicole Bazuin and me, is a four-part video investigation into the love lives of accomplished Canadians, starring Wayson Choy, Atom Egoyan, Bette Logan, and Dan Hill, with the Torontonians – Virginia Antonipillai, Sanjay Ratnan, Daniel Lastres Rodrigues, Kathy Vuu, and Wendell Williams – firing hardball questions at the celebs.
- *A Drift in Gloucester,* presented by JOLT International Theatre Festival, featured a number of the Torontonians/Young Mammals collaborating with youth from two Gloucester, U.K., youth arts organizations. The young people drifted around the city and offered to help random people, then took to the stage to report on their findings, in the first of what is now a growing series of ethnographic performances.

2015

- *The AGO Youth Receptiveness Assessment Initiative* was part of our Art Gallery of Ontario residency – we assessed the gallery's potential permeability to young people according to the principles in the Succession Model for Youth Labour Engagement. In collaboration with the Torontonians, the Young Mammalians, and members of the AGO Youth Council, we met and interviewed forty staff members, did some socializing with them, and canvassed and surveyed the surrounding neighbourhood to study nearby youth and their interests.
- *Textures of Toronto,* conceived by Sanjay Ratnan, was an investigation of the various textures of nine Toronto neighbourhoods. With the guidance of local residents, the young people collected samples of local ephemera, plant life, debris, a lobster carcass, and other materials specific to the neighbourhood. The survey cumulated in an installation of over one hundred jars representing the different urban systems of the city as part of the Gladstone Hotel's Grow Op exhibition.
- *Teen Thoughts*, conceived and directed by Nicole Bazuin, and written by me from interviews with the performers, was a short film featuring five members of the Torontonians and Young Mammals: Sanjay Ratnan, Virginia Antonipillai, Sharay Dennis, Tenzin Chozin, and Kathy Vuu, who quietly dished on what it is to be human. It was commissioned by the CBC, is part of the Collective, and can be

viewed at www.cbc.ca/arts/thecollective/the-collective-mammalian-diving-reflex-1.3106507.

- *Teens Talk Theatre*, an adaptation of *The Children's Choice Awards*, was an ongoing youth residency at the Theatre Centre that culminated in an award ceremony lauding the season's best performances.

2016

Teentalitarianism was first presented by the Ruhrtriennale Festival and created in collaboration with the Torontonians, the Young Mammals, and Mit Ohne Alles; it is a touring vehicle for training the Toronto youth in the entire cycle of event production, from first contact with a presenter to delivering the project on the ground. *Teentalitarianism* features a number of the projects created with the Torontonians from 2010 to 2015, as well as a couple of projects conceived for the collective but never realized, and two new projects designed specifically for the Ruhrtriennale. In the inaugural production, *Teentalitarianism* took over the festival centre, a large and complex installation designed by Dutch architecture firm Atellier Van Leishout, with the youth given residency in of one of the spaces: a trailer originally designed for the Walker Art Centre as a mobile art lab for youth.

- *Rules of the Teen State and Visas* – For several of the *Teentalitarianism* events, the adults were required to apply for a visa through an interview to determine how teen-friendly they were. Those who scored low were permitted in the space for only a short period of time before having to reapply.
- *What the Kids Found on the Internet* featured both German and Canadian youth counting backward from age seventeen to age five and screening extreme internet content they've stumbled across over the years. The content was then discussed with media psychologist Max Braun, as he and the teens talked about the social purpose of the content as well as the effects on the youth.
- *Nightwalks with Teenagers*, in this version, explored the post-industrial area around Bochum's Westpark.
- *Jugensongs* was a live music performance featuring the songs written by the Torontonians during the 2012 *Grilled Open Cheese Office Songwriting Sandwich*, as well as songs written by Mit Ohne Alles in the months preceding the festival.
- *Ask for the Moon* was the culminating presentation following a series of closed-door meetings with the Toronto and German youth to

create a series of demands for their future involvement with Mammalian and the Ruhrtriennale. The performance featured a negotiation between me, the youth, Ruhrtriennale director Johan Simons, and managing director Lukas Crepas to determine which demands we would all agree to. Interestingly, their demands required an increased commitment on their part, something we had been trying to galvanize with mixed results over the previous year. By successfully extracting a series of commitments from us, they, in turn, had to make commitments to us. For example, their demand for a higher-profile project in the festival necessitated a commitment on their part to participate in a devising process over the course of the year.

- *Dare Night* took place in the largest space within the Good, the Bad and the Ugly, the Refektorium.
- *Jahrhundertspiele* was a series of games played outside the Jahrhunderthalle performance space as the audiences for the various events sipped on their pre-show wine.

Two of the *Teentalitarianism* projects involved the German youth alone:
- *Sexualkunde* was a live German-language version of the film project *High School Health* and featured the teenagers interviewing festival luminaries, including festival director Johan Simons, about their romantic histories.
- *Snapped* was a short dramatic thriller shot entirely with the app Snapchat on the teens' many phones. It was directed by Jana Eiting and edited by Konstantin Bock.

Teentalitarianism will be presented in upcoming festivals in Italy and the U.K., and is now a part of Mammalian's touring repertoire, as a site for training the Torontonians and Young Mammals, as we deliver and improve upon the many projects we created together.

- *Wisdoms*, conceived and directed by Eva Verity, is an intergenerational podcast created in collaboration with Brainchild Podcasts, featuring Parkdale youth along with seniors living in a long-term care facility in Toronto's west end. *Wisdoms* brought teens and older adults together to shoot the shit about love, life, and run-ins with the law.

2017
Teentalitarianism 2017
The 2017 iteration of *Teentalitarianism* at the Ruhrtriennale repeated the most successful of the 2016 projects, including *SexualKunde*, retitled by the youth *Sex, Drugs and Criminality*, expanding the focus from romance to include other popular transgressions; *Nightwalks with Teenagers*, performed in Duisberg, the home city of the second wave of young people to join the German collective Mit Ohne Alles; and a new version of *Snapped*, its format updated from dramatic thriller to a documentary about the world of cosplay. *Handies in the Hands of Teens*, conceived by Cathrin Rose, was an instructional performance sharing the teen's knowledge of cellphones.

Happy Eatium
Conceived by Eva Verity and Ana-Marija Stojic and directed by Tijana Spasic, *Happy Eatium* featured teens from four different neighbourhoods assessing the food they are most drawn to, taking into consideration cost, convenience, taste, and healthiness. They explored their food habits, talked to a nutritionist, made a zine filled with data and recipes: their own, their families', and those stolen from restaurants they liked best. The project culminated in four meals and presentations in each area of the city.

Mammalian's Work with Mit Ohne Alles

Mit Ohne Alles is a youth collective in the Ruhr region of Germany that was spun off from Mammalian's three years of *The Children's Choice Awards* (2012–2015) at the Ruhrtriennale Festival, and includes young people from the cities Bochum and Duisburg.

2014
Small Talk in Daft Hell
Small Talk in Daft Hell was a performance devised with Mit Ohne Alles that took off from the question of how the young people wanted to frighten and, in turn, console an adult audience. A theatre-based project, it guided the audience throughout the many rooms of PACT Zollverein, an historic colliery in Essen, Germany.

2015

Millionen! Millionen! Millionen!

Millionen! Millionen! Millionen! was a performance created in response to Mit Ohne Alles's desire to work with more marginalized young people, in particular recent immigrants and refugees to the region. We used methods based in ethnographic performance and went camping with the two groups of youth, and then together 'reported' on what happened during this moment of social acupuncture. Subsequently several of the newer youth joined Mit Ohne Alles and have continued to work with us.

Teentalitarianism (2016 and 2017)

Teentalitarianism was created in collaboration with Mit Ohne Alles and the Torontonians/Young Mammals for the Ruhrtriennale Festival and is described above.

The intention is to train the young people in Germany on existing projects, tour the projects we devise with them, weave them together with the Toronto youth as well as the London youth outlined below, and facilitate their collaboration with other cultural organizations in the U.K., Germany, Canada, and anywhere else we can manage.

The Tottenham UpLIFTers

Co-directed with Alice Fleming, the Tottenham UpLIFTers is a collaboration between the London International Festival of Theatre and two schools in Tottenham, London: Northumberland Park Community School and the Vale, whose students have a range of special educational needs. Modelled after the work in Parkdale, this collaboration features five years of increasingly deep engagement with the young people and is the first comprehensive application of the SMYLE outside of Mammalian.

Year one (2015–2016) featured visits to the school by nine artists living in Tottenham – Jeremy Carne, Imwen Eke, Keren Ghitis, Güneş Güvenify, Kazuko Hoki, Theodora Omambala, and Louis Parker-Evans – who delivered an after-school arts experience. The year culminated in a presentation of *The Children's Choice Awards* at the 2016 LIFT Festival.

Year two (2016–2017), *Live from High Street*, featured four projects created in collaboration with the artists, the students, and businesses along the Tottenham High Street. Theo Omambala worked with Chicken Town, Tottenham's social enterprise chicken shop, and local eco designer Jose Hendo to create a flash mob dance. Güneş Güvenify and Elsabet

Yonas worked with record store Body Music, and co-designed a creative protest and march. Imwen Eke worked in conjunction with Body Music, Chicken Town, and Bernie Grant Arts Centre on a geo-locative game. Kazuko Hohki, brought in three speakers – a very optimistic real estate agent, a member of the local council, and a representative from an anti-regeneration group – to discuss the gentrification affecting the neighbourhood, then worked with the young people to design their ideal neighbourhoods, the models of which were presented on the Tottenham High Street. Each project occurred over the course of five weeks and included a site visit, three development sessions, a dress rehearsal, and a weekend performance.

Year three (2017–2018) is a yearlong exploration of the cultural landscape of London through regular field trips to see performance work and meet artists, presenters, and other luminaries and heavyweights in London's culture industries. Additionally, the young people will be researching the city for their preferred location for *Nightwalks with Teenagers*, which will be presented by LIFT in the 2018 festival. The year will also begin to include the youth's participation on panels, public presentations, and talks, as they build their skills at communicating their experiences during the initiative.

Year four (2018–2019) reproduces the Toronto project *Producers of Parkdale*, as the youth attend formal workshops and learn about event production from LIFT staff and associates, with continued participation on panels, public presentations, and talks.

Year five (2019–2020) features the creation of an original performance work to be presented in the 2020 LIFT Festival and continues the youth's participation on panels, public presentations, and talks.

Beyond the five-year engagement, as with the work with the Young Mammals and Mit Ohne Alles, the intention is to train the young people on existing projects, tour the projects we devise with them, weave the three groups of young people together, and facilitate their collaboration with other cultural organizations in the U.K., Germany, Canada, and anywhere else we can manage.

Mammalian Diving Reflex's Other Work with Children

Collaboration with the Horizons Youth Ambassadors Program at Upper Canada College (2009)

The Horizons Youth Ambassadors program at UCC works with students from Toronto's public school system, offering them mentoring opportunities. Mammalian introduced an innovation into the program by inviting the students to put forward a material aspect of Toronto they would like to change – they chose to green Dundas Square. In response, Mammalian and UCC organized a series of social opportunities for the students to meet and pick the brains of people we all felt could help them realize their goal. The project featured skills-building, good times, network-building, and city improvement all rolled into one.

Monster Makers (2011)

Monster Makers was a stage-based performance developed in collaboration with the children of the Mumbai-based Aarambh; Tasmania's Streets Alive Youth Festival; and Contact Inc, Brisbane, and was presented at Toronto's Harbourfront Centre (2011), the Magnetic North Theatre Festival (2011), and the National Arts Centre (2012). The project started from a simple game in Mumbai where children worked with an actor to turn him into a monster and take him on a walk through their community. *Monster Makers* then evolved into a scripted participatory performance for children featuring a Sad Scientist who – much to his chagrin – has accidentally created a Friendly Monster. The Sad Scientist turns to the children in the audience to help him teach the Friendly Monster how to be a Monstrous Monster, then take him outside to terrify the public.

Years of testing and working with the different groups of children produced reliable methods for turning the children themselves into monsters during the performance, as the responsibility the kids took quickly morphed into authoritarianism. The show concludes with a dissuasion led by the sobbing scientist about why his request that the children 'take care' of the monster had so quickly morphed into the children oppressing and, ultimately, alienating the monster, forcing him to flee to rediscover his freedom and autonomy.

These Are the People in Your Neighbourhood (2012)

These Are the People in Your Neighbourhood was first presented by Art of the Danforth and Jane's Walk. Groups of ten-year-olds from Dovercourt

Public School and R. H. McGregor Elementary School met and interviewed the owner-operators of local small businesses, created a guide to these people and their places, then introduced them through a neighbourhood tour. *These Are the People in Your Neighbourhood* is a positive street-proofing and community fortification performance led by children and fuelled by their curiosity about the world and their enthusiasm to share it. It is a performance of a very possible world: a place where children walk down the street, tipping their hats to the people they pass and making it safe and familiar for everyone. *These Are the People in Your Neighbourhood* continues to tour and has been presented in Adelaide, Gwangju, Helsinki, Knislinge, Reading, and Toronto.

Future Tastes of Toronto: At The Kids' Table (2013)

Future Tastes of Toronto: At the Kids' Table, presented by the Luminato Festival, was an adaptation of *These Are the People in Your Neighbourhood*. Instead of meeting owner-operators of businesses local to their school, *Future Tastes of Toronto: At the Kids' Table* brought students from Dovercourt Public School, Duke of Connaught Junior and Senior Public School, George Peck Public School, Lord Dufferin Junior and Senior Public School, and Rose Avenue Junior Public School together with twenty chefs in Toronto's Distillery District. The young people got to know the chefs, created a bunch of menu items, then, during the performance, the kids shared their behind-the-scenes knowledge about the chefs and the food being presented in a communal eating area.

THE MAMMALIAN PROTOCOL FOR COLLABORATING WITH CHILDREN AND YOUNG PEOPLE

Dedication

The Mammalian Protocol for Collaborating with Children is dedicated to a few key people.

First up are all the children we've worked with: you guys are great, your participation has rocked the company's foundation and provided us with a reason – beyond art – to exist – and we will be eternally grateful.

Second, we dedicate this to Ernie Boulton, the principal who first gave us the green light to work with his students at Parkdale Public School in Toronto, staring at us sternly across his desk and demanding, 'What's in it for them?'

Third, we dedicate it to the students at a school in Europe, which, after a week of working with us, dropped out of the project because it was 'too complicated' for the kids. The crew of resilient ten-year-olds responded with a confident 'Um, actually, we're not dropping the project … we like it.' The significant thing about this group of kids is that they are not particularly extraordinary, and it's our belief that they acted like any children who had unilaterally and without consultation been denied participation in a project they deemed worthy – and we love them for that.

Finally, we dedicate this protocol to that teacher who tried to yank the plug on our project, acknowledging that what we are proposing is daunting and there is no shame in being afraid: children are often afraid.

Introduction

Performance company Mammalian Diving Reflex has developed a rights-based approach to artistic collaborations with children, using the *United Nations Convention on the Rights of the Child* (the Convention), *Implementation Handbook for the Convention on the Rights of the Child* (the *Handbook*), the Universal Declaration on Human Rights, the International Covenant on Civil and Political Rights, and Declaration of the Child's Right to Play as primary resources upon which we base our methodology. Using the Convention as framework, in particular articles 5, 12, 13, 15, 19, 29, 30, 31, 32, and 36, the company has developed specific protocols for dealing with common situations when collaborating with children and the institutions in which children are most commonly engaged, including the family, schools, community, cultural centres, and arts organizations.

This protocol is a summary of the child's rights relevant to our collaborations with children and the institutions in which they are engaged, both in terms of our desires and expectations with respect to how the children are to be treated while collaborating with us, but also with respect to the underlying artistic themes of the projects. All of our collaborations with children have, at one level or another, the theme of the full recognition of children as rights holders who are 'not only entitled to receive protection but also have the right to participate in all matters affecting them, a right which can be considered as the symbol for their recogniton as rights holders. This implies, in the long term, changes in political, social, institutional and cultural structures'; in effect, 'a new social contract.'[73]

Mammalian Diving Reflex's artistic projects with children are attempts at utopian moments that offer the possibility of seeing children differently and accepting their presence, energy, and disruptive potential as important reminders that, perhaps, we are all taking things a little too seriously, moving a little too fast, and expecting too much of each other. We are concerned that the social norms and codes of professionalism that exclude or prove challenging to children – things as simple as the expectation of complete silence while watching a theatre performance or the prohibition against exuberant play while in most public spaces – are norms and codes that are too restrictive even for adults. Taking, as an example, the expectation of silence during a theatre performance, we find that the codes of behaviour demanded of the audience are historical and cultural constructions, and, at other times and in other places, the role of the audience was very different, with an expectation and acceptance of boisterous participation.[74]

Facilitating the presence of children in a much wider range of activities and accepting this presence on their terms, without the vigilant controlling of their impulses that we currently accept as the norm, is seen as a possible avenue for establishing a new sort of generosity in the public sphere, not only between adults and children, but between adults themselves. For example, when we present our project *Eat the Street* – featuring a jury of children food critics travelling to restaurants and offering their opinion of the food – we have noticed that the pressure on the servers to deal with a large group of children is accepted by the adults, who handle the compromised service with good-humoured equanimity, in contrast to the high levels of professionalism expected and the irritation that occurs when it is an adults-only environment. The *Handbook* also observes, 'Children are capable of playing a unique role in bridging differences that have historically separated groups of people.'[75] It is this generosity and acceptance of our beautifully flawed humanity that we feel the presence of children can provide for everyone, but to do this we need, as the Committee on the Rights of the Child has observed, a 'new social contract'[76] with 'long term changes in political, social, institutional and cultural structures.'[77] Mammalian Diving Reflex's tagline is 'ideal entertainment for the end of world,' by which we mean 'this' world, rife as it is with inequity, violence, war, environmental devastation, and greed, with the hope for a world that is fair and generous. Our modest strategy toward actualizing this future is the simple gesture of including children as rights holders and, in addition to providing them responsible protection and guidance, according them a set of rights and freedoms in all matters affecting them.

Mammalian Diving Reflex, while dedicated to a thorough application of the Convention, understands that life is more complicated than international treaties and that occasionally – even often – there are circumstances where a pure application of the Convention may compromise the child's rights or the rights of a majority of the children. We feel a thorough understanding of the aspects of the Convention related to our collaborations is important as a foundation upon which to foster discussion and facilitate communication, and that negotiations are expected to be constant, never-ending, with compromise and the understanding of each other's – often complicated – position being key.

The United Nations Convention on the Rights of the Child

The United Nations Convention on the Rights of the Child is a human rights treaty setting out the civil, political, economic, social, health, and cultural rights of children. The Convention defines a child as any human being under the age of eighteen, unless an earlier age of majority is recognized by a country's law.

Nations that ratify this Convention are bound to it by international law. Compliance is monitored by the United Nations Committee on the Rights of the Child, which is composed of members from countries around the world. Once a year, the UNCRC submits a report to the Third Committee of the United Nations General Assembly, which also hears a statement from the CRC chair, and the assembly adopts a Resolution on the Rights of the Child.

Governments of countries that have ratified the Convention are periodically required to report to, and appear before, the UNCRC, to be examined on their progress with regards to the advancement of the implementation of the Convention and the status of child rights in their country. Their reports and the committee's written views and concerns are available on the committee's website.

The United Nations General Assembly adopted the Convention and opened it for signature on November 20, 1989. It came into force on September 2, 1990, after the required number of nations ratified it. As of November 2009, 194 countries have ratified it, including every member of the United Nations except Somalia and the United States of America. Somalia's cabinet ministers have announced plans to ratify the treaty.

Mammalian Diving Reflex has identified a number of articles as having particularly strong relevance to our collaborations with children and the institutions in which they are engaged and that engage them: Article 5: Parental Guidance and the Child's Evolving Capacities; Article 12: Respect for the Views of the Child; Article 13: Child's Right to Freedom of Expression; Article 15: Child's Right to Freedom of Association and Peaceful Assembly; Article 19: Child's Right to Protection from All Forms of Violence; Article 29: The Aims of Education; Article 30: Children of Minorities and Indigenous People; Article 31: Child's Right to Leisure, Play and Culture; Article 32: Child Labour; and Article 36: Child's Right to Protection from Other Forms of Exploitation.

The Mammalian Protocol for Collaborating with Children

Each relevant article of UNCRC and its relevance to Mammalian Diving Reflex is briefly introduced in an executive summary. The full protocol with the entirety of each relevant article of the Convention is then presented, followed by a detailed explanation of what Mammalian Diving Reflex considers the important aspects for our purposes and their practical implications and applications.

Article 5: Parental Guidance and the Child's Evolving Capacities

States Parties shall respect the responsibilities, rights and duties of parents or, where applicable, the members of the extended family or community as provided for by local custom, legal guardians, or other persons legally responsible for the child, to provide, in a manner consistent with the evolving capacities of the child, appropriate direction and guidance in the exercise by the child of the rights recognized in the present Convention.

The *Handbook* points out that the 'Convention regards the child as the active subject of rights, emphasizing the exercise "by the child" of his or her rights,'[78] and that the Committee on the Rights of the Child (the Committee) has noted that 'the rights and prerogatives of the parents may not undermine the rights of the child as recognized by the Convention, especially the right of the child to express his or her own views and that his or her views be given due weight'[79] and that 'with regards to parenthood, the emphasis should not be on authority but on responsibility.'[80]

The implications of this are that we are vigilant about not commanding the children and telling them what to do and what not to do. Our responsibility to the children is to protect them from any potential harm, but, within the parameters of our projects, we do not assume any authority to dictate their behaviour except insofar as their behaviour may cause them or others harm or infringe on the rights of others.

A very common scenario is the impulse to dictate and control behaviour based on the social disturbances the children may be causing people external to the projects. We do not consider this to constitute 'harm to others' and take the position that if the children are disturbing someone, we either let that person deal with it themselves or we express to the child that their behaving is making us uncomfortable. We do not presume to speak for the member of the public but, rather, we take responsibility for our own feelings on the matter and allow the child to then take responsibility for the discomfort their actions are causing us and correct their behaviour accordingly.

We do not take a position of authority over the child and we ask all participating institutions to do the same.

Article 12: Respect for the Views of the Child

1. States Parties shall assure to the child who is capable of forming his or her own views the right to express those views freely in all matters affecting the child, the views of the child being given due weight in accordance with the age and maturity of the child.

2. For this purpose, the child shall in particular be provided the opportunity to be heard in any judicial and administrative proceedings affecting the child, either directly, or through a representative or an appropriate body, in a manner consistent with the procedural rules of national law.

This right is in accordance with the Universal Declaration of Human Rights, which states: 'Everyone has the right to freedom of opinion and expression; this right includes freedom to hold opinions without interference and to seek, receive and impart information and ideas through any media and regardless of frontiers.'[81] And the International Covenant on Civil and Political Rights states: 'Everyone shall have the right to hold opinions without interference.'[82]

Mammalian Diving Reflex is in agreement with the Committee's statement 'A shift away from traditional beliefs that regard early childhood mainly as a period for the socialization of the immature human being towards mature adult status is required. The Convention requires that children, including the very youngest children, be respected as persons in their own right. Young children should be recognized as active members of families, communities and societies, with their own concerns, interests and points of view.'[83]

The children, no matter how young and to what extent their views or actions may be interpreted as 'immature,' are respected as persons in their own right and are not corrected. We may offer an opinion on their behaviour, but we are vigilant about making it clear that our opinion is simply our opinion.

The implications of these ideas for Mammalian are that we welcome the full participation of children to hold whatever views they like, insofar as it does not infringe on the rights of any other person – child or otherwise. Therefore, we do not view our role or the function of the project to be one of correcting the children toward higher levels of 'maturity,' or to teach them any sort of etiquette or modes of social behaviour that are considered more 'correct' for a given circumstance. We share our opinions on these matters with them, but we do not impose particular behaviours or prohibit others.

Article 13: The Child's Right to Freedom of Expression

1. The child shall have the right to freedom of expression; this right shall include freedom to seek, receive, and impart information and ideas of all kinds, regardless of frontiers, either orally, in writing, or in print, in the form of art, or through any other media of the child's choice.

2. The exercise of this right may be subject to certain restrictions, but these shall only be such as are provided by law and are necessary: (a) For respect of the rights or reputations of others; or (b) For the protection of national security or of public order (ordre public), or of public health or morals.

Following directly on the child's right to respect for their views is the child's right to be free to express these views, a right accorded everyone in both the Universal Declaration of Human Rights and the International Covenant on Civil and Political Rights.

Some of our projects bring the children in contact with members of the public, where the young people's method of expressing their views may have an adverse effect on other people's – or, for that matter, our – enjoyment of an event. To the extent it is possible, we make every effort to facilitate communication between the offended adult and the offending child so that the child is aware of the effects of his or her actions, but we try not to restrict those actions, having learned from experience that when a child is informed that their behaviour is causing distress, they are generally able to take responsibility and more or less monitor themselves. We apply the same principle to our interactions with the child and refrain from telling them how to behave, but rather, we inform them how their behaviour is making us feel and allow them the opportunity to take responsibility. Therefore we regard 'shushing' or commanding the children to do or stop doing something to be an infringement of Articles 12 and 13.

We understand this may sound like an overzealous application of the Convention but feel it is reflective of the previously referenced 'new social contract,' which 'implies, in the long term, changes in political, social, institutional and cultural structures,'[84] which, it should be pointed out, are bound to feel strange, particularly in a traditional institutional setting like a school. However, the Committee is very clear that 'there are no boundaries on the obligation of States Parties to assure the child the right to express views freely. In particular, this emphasizes that there is no area of traditional parental or adult authority – the home or school for example – in which children's views have no place.'[85] Therefore we consider the child's right to express their point of view to be something we allow in whatever form that may take.

Technology

The use of technology can sometimes be challenging during our projects, when the children are more captivated by their phones and the texts they are sending and receiving than by what we are offering them. However, we feel the onus is on us to provide activities more interesting than the games on their phones and, if we do not, this is our failure, not theirs. The Committee emphasizes that media 'offers children the possibility of expressing themselves.'[86] In the report of its General Discussion on 'The child and the media,' the Committee promoted children's participatory rights in relation to the media. 'The Internet and modern information and communications technology, including mobile phones, provide children with new opportunities to seek and impart information regardless of frontiers or adult restrictions.'[87]

In the event the child's activities disrupt our activities, we respond by informing the children of our feelings and allow them the opportunity to take responsibility for their actions. We do not command them to put away any electronic technology, and we do not confiscate it.

Play

The *Handbook* makes the point that 'of particular importance to children's freedom of expression is the right to engage in play,'[88] which is also supported by Article 31: Child's Right to Leisure, Play and Culture. For us, this means the child's impulse to play should be respected irrespective of the perceived appropriateness of this activity or any disruption it may cause.

In the event the child's play disrupts our activities, we respond by informing the children of our feelings and allow them the opportunity to take responsibility for their actions. We do not command the children to stop playing or control any manifestations of physical exuberance.

Bullying

The right to freedom of expression, however, is accompanied by the restrictions that are necessary 'for respect of the rights or reputations of others.'[89] While this restriction is something the Convention states 'shall only be such that as are provided by law,' the Committee recognizes the damaging role of bullying.[90] Therefore, we feel the right to expression is restricted in the case of bullying, notwithstanding the fact that the prohibition against bullying is not a restriction that is provided by law.

Parental Guidance

Article 5: Parental Guidance and the Child's Evolving Capacities states that parents and others have the 'responsibilities, rights and duties to provide, in a manner consistent with the evolving capacities of the child, appropriate direction and guidance in the exercise by the child of (their) rights.'[91] This role for parents is repeated in Article 14: Child's Right to Freedom of Thought, Conscience and Religion. However, this is not the case in Article 13: The Child's Right to Freedom of Expression or 15: The Child's Right to Freedom of Association and Peaceful Assembly.[92] The implications of this for us are that, while guidance is expected in the exercising of the rights in general and in the exercising of the right to freedom of thought, conscience, and religion, it is considered less relevant in the case of the right to expression, association, and peaceful assembly, and therefore the child's right to these is more important than the parent's or other guardian's desire to guide them in a particular direction.

Swearing

We respect the right of the institution to impose sanctions on the act of swearing, while at the same time doubting the efficacy of these prohibitions, believing that to forbid is to make attractive. We regard swearing as a minor infraction of social codes with a double standard that favours adults. Most thoroughly successful adults indulged in swearing as a child, and many still do as adults, with no repercussions for their moral code: they were and remain good people. Mammalian Diving Reflex regards swears, in and of themselves, silly words that only gain power as something said that is not supposed to be said and view them as symptomatic of many of the strange contradictions hovering around our social being.

When working with young people on our own terms, we choose to tailor our language according to the limits set by the children and, if they swear, to the extent that we might use the same word, we do. However we do not swear in the presence of the child, unless they swear in the presence of us and we do so only insofar as we would swear in the presence of an adult – that is, we don't go out of our way to swear but we don't pretend to be angels, if the young people have set a less than angelic standard.

School Uniform

The intention of the Mammalian Protocol is not to intervene in a given institution's treatment of children but to note that when the institution and Mammalian Diving Reflex share responsibility for the child, we prefer the children to be treated according to the terms established in the Convention. Therefore, for example, we do not request that a given institution change its approach to the children when the children are in their sole care or on their property, but when we are not at the given institution, we do not oblige the children to dress in any particular way – for example, allowing them to choose their attire, particularly when we are participating in a public event such as an award ceremony, where we consider the comfort of the child to be a priority over etiquette.

We note that there are extenuating circumstances where the obligation to wear a school uniform, for example, is designed to reduce pressure on the economically deprived child and we are open to negotiating these situations on a case-by-case basis.

Health and Safety

Invoking notions of health and safety is a common strategy for controlling and invading the privacy of populations in the case of both adults and children. This is particularly relevant to the child's right to express themselves through play, with declarations of danger used to curtail simple disruption. While the health and safety of all of our collaborators – be they children or adults – is a priority taking precedence above all other, we regard the invocation of health and safety as very serious and consider their arbitrary and opportunistic use, designed to simply control the children for behaviour deemed disruptive, to be a violation of the children's rights of expression and right to play (Article 31, below).

Article 15: Child's Right to Freedom of Assembly

1. *States Parties recognize the rights of the child to freedom of association and to freedom of peaceful assembly.*
2. *No restrictions may be placed on the exercise of these rights other than those imposed in conformity with the law and which are necessary in a democratic society in the interests of national security or public safety, public order, the protection of public health or morals, or the protection of the rights and freedoms of others.*

Article 15 is clear that children have the right to associate with whomever they want and that 'no restrictions may be placed upon this right, except those in conformity with the law and … in the interests of national security or public safety, public order, the protection of public health or morals or the protection of the rights and freedoms of others.'

Considering the widespread concern regarding the protection of children and, in particular, the possible exposure to sexual exploitation, the *Handbook* observes the child has this freedom of association with other individuals as long as the 'individual does not threaten the child's other rights, including to protection.'[93]

Article 15 is of particular interest to arts organizations like Mammalian Diving Reflex who create works that bring children and adults together to participate in events and consider the right to protection to be the highest priority. We recognize, however, that the rights outlined in Article 19: The Child's Right to Protection from All Forms of Violence do consider it important to acknowledge the difficult fact that the vast majority of incidents of abuse are perpetrated not by strangers or other individuals, such as artists, who have minimal and occasional contact with the child but by family members or other persons related to the child who, according to The *Canadian Incidence Study of Reported Child Abuse and Neglect*, constitute the vast majority (93 per cent) of perpetrators.[94] American, British, and Australian studies present similar findings.[95]

Background Checks

While difficult to acknowledge, it is crucial to point out the terrible fact that it is when we say goodbye and send the child home at the conclusion of each day's collaborative activities that we should be concerned about the child's safety, and not so much during their participation with our projects, where the child is more likely to be safe.

In some cases, policy exists that requires arts organizations working with vulnerable persons including children to submit employees and volunteers to a criminal background check. Mammalian Diving Reflex's staff complies with this request and we have had our records checked in Canada, but believe that restricting the child's association only to those individuals who have submitted to this check is an infringement on the child's right to freedom of association and, considering the facts outlined above, does nothing to address the site and situation of the vast majority of abuses.

Board Participation

Mammalian Diving Reflex takes a particularly keen interest in the *Handbook*'s flagging of the fact that full implementation of Article 15 faces an impediment when considering laws concerning the child's right to act as directors or trustees of public associations.[96] Though they are not entitled by law to vote, we include teenagers on our Board of Directors whose opinions we consider before making any decisions. The *Handbook* also notes that some States require children to garner the agreement of their parents before joining associations, but that 'the Convention provides no support for arbitrary limitations on the child's right to freedom of association.'[97]

Friendship

In terms of the child's association with peers, we respect their right to freedom of association and will not separate students who want to spend time with or sit next to each other. In the event their association is leading to behaviour that is disrupting our activities, we, again, respond by informing the child of our feelings and allow them the opportunity to take responsibility for their actions. We acknowledge that peer pressure to participate in activities that are disruptive can overwhelm some children and lead to undesired participation, so we make efforts to recognize this and encourage peers to work in different pairs or groups while offering a variety of participatory options to address this.

Online/Facebook

In terms of online association, Mammalian Diving Reflex utilizes online forums for communicating and collaborating with young people, including blogs and social media such as Facebook, Snapchat, Instagram, Twitter, and WhatsApp. Facebook has proven to be a particularly effective tool for remaining in touch and fostering ongoing collaborations with children and young people from locations we may not have the opportunity to visit regularly. Mammalian Diving Reflex takes the long view, and is building an international network of children and young people who have collaborated with the company in order to foster further collaborations that we intend to continue as the child makes their way into adulthood, providing employment, travel, and professional development opportunities. Currently there is one twenty-year-old woman we have known since she was eleven who we have engaged as a project coordinator and sent to Europe to begin training on our projects. We will foster this sort of relationship with as many children as we can over the years, eventually engaging them as project initiators, and lead artists, and, ultimately, ceding the company to them when we are ready to retire. It is our artistic goal for the company to eventually be led by an artistic directorship of individuals who we began working with when they were children. Facebook and other social media are central to our ability to accomplish this.

Thought vs. Expression

As was observed in the previous article, Article 5: Parental Guidance and the Child's Evolving Capacities states that parents and others have the 'responsibilities, rights and duties to provide, in a manner consistent with the evolving capacities of the child, appropriate direction and guidance in the exercise by the child of (their) rights.'[98] This role for parents is repeated in Article 14: Child's Right to Freedom of Thought, Conscience and Religion but not in Articles 13: The Child's Right to Freedom of Expression or 15: The Child's Right to Freedom of Association and Peaceful Assembly.[99] The implications of this for us are that, while guidance is expected in the exercising of the rights in general and in the exercising of the right to freedom of thought, conscience, and religion, it is considered less relevant in the case of the right to expression, association, and peaceful assembly; therefore the child's right to these is more important than the parent's desire to guide them in a particular direction.

Article 19: Child's Protection from All Forms of Violence

1. States Parties shall take all appropriate legislative, administrative, social, and educational measures to protect the child from all forms of physical or mental violence, injury or abuse, neglect or negligent treatment, maltreatment or exploitation, including sexual abuse, while in the care of parent(s), legal guardian(s), or any other person who has the care of the child.

2. Such protective measures should, as appropriate, include effective procedures for the establishment of social programs to provide necessary support for the child and for those who have the care of the child, as well as for other forms of prevention and for identification, reporting, referral, investigation, treatment, and follow-up of instances of child maltreatment described heretofore, and, as appropriate, for judicial involvement.

Article 15 is clear that children have the right to associate with whomever they want and that 'no restrictions may be placed upon this right, except those in conformity with the law and … in the interests of national security or public safety, public order, the protection of public health or morals or the protection of the rights and freedoms of others.'

Considering the widespread concern regarding the protection of children and, in particular, the possible exposure to sexual exploitation, the *Handbook* observes the child has this freedom of association with other individuals as long as the 'individual does not threaten the child's other rights, including to protection.'[100]

Article 15 is of particular interest to arts organizations like Mammalian Diving Reflex who create works that bring children and adults together to participate in events and consider the right to protection to be the highest priority. We recognize, however, that the rights outlined in Article 19: The Child's Right to Protection from All Forms of Violence do consider it important to acknowledge the difficult fact that the vast majority of incidents of abuse are perpetrated not by strangers or other individuals, such as artists, who have minimal and occasional contact with the child but *by family members or other persons related to the child* who, according to *The Canadian Incidence Study of Reported Child Abuse and Neglect*, constitute the vast majority (93 per cent) of perpetrators.[101] American, British, and Australian studies present similar findings.[102]

The *Handbook* states, 'Article 19 requires children's protection from "all forms of physical or mental violence" while in the care of parents or others. Thus, Article 19 asserts children's equal human right to full respect for their dignity and physical and personal integrity.'[103]

Mental Violence and Humiliation

While Mammalian Diving Reflex acknowledges the gravity of physical violence suffered by children, it is the more common occurrence of mental violence that we are sensitive to in our projects, acknowledging that 'there are other non-physical forms of punishment which are also cruel and degrading and thus incompatible with the Convention. These include, for example, punishments that belittle, humiliate, denigrate, scapegoat, threaten, scare or ridicule the child.[104] Mammalian Diving Reflex does not utilize any forms of humiliation and considers the other various infringements on the rights of the child, particularly when occurring in a public way in front of peers, to be a form of humiliation and therefore an infringement of Article 19. Yelling at the children in front of their peers, yelling at them to 'be quiet' or 'shut up,' are also considered acts of violence in that they are direct infringements of Article 13: Child's Right to Freedom of Expression.

Representation
We consider the child to be strictly a representative of theirself and do not assign to the child the responsibility of representing Mammalian Diving Reflex or any institution we are working with. The child is our collaborator who has agreed to create with us, but their behaviour is not seen as a reflection of our abilities or aptitude. We therefore consider statements that suggest the child is 'representing the school' or any other organization to be incorrect and, ultimately, coercive. While we may feel self-conscious that the child is acting in a particular way, we do not consider this a reflection on us, and if other people consider us lacking in any way and view us or our partner organizations negatively, we simply accept this with equanimity and as one of the costs of facilitating the full rights of the child. To the extent that the child's behaviour is causing distress to others, including ourselves, we bring this to the attention of the child but we do not assign to the child the responsibility of representing entities other than themselves.

Right to Food
The Committee on Economic, Social and Cultural Rights notes: 'Other aspects of school discipline may also be inconsistent with human dignity, such as public humiliation. Nor should any form of discipline breach other rights under the Covenant, such as the right to food.'[105] Therefore threats to deprive the children of snacks until they start behaving in a particular way are considered infringements of Article 19.

Access to Friends
The *Handbook* states, 'Corporal punishment is not the only form of school discipline to breach Article 28: Child's Right to Education); public humiliation, for instance, is not consistent with the child's human dignity,'[106] and the Committee has noted that other forms of cruel punishment include 'punishment which belittles, humiliates, denigrates, scapegoats, threatens, scares or ridicules the child.'[107] The *Handbook* continues, ' … and care should be taken not to violate other rights under the Convention. For example, punishments that stop children's access to their friends would be in breach of rights under the Convention

and of article 28(2).'[108] Therefore we do not separate children from their friends to correct for behaviour that is disruptive. Again, we explain to the children the effects of their actions on us and allow them to take responsibility.

A Note with Respect to the U.K.

In its initial report to the Committee on the Rights of the Child, the United Kingdom stated that 'appropriate direction and guidance' of the child 'include the administration, by the parent, of reasonable and moderate physical chastisement to a child.'[109] However, the Committee on the Rights of the Child has stated that 'there is no place for corporeal punishment' and that 'the Committee is clear that parental "guidance" must not take the form of violent or humiliating discipline, as the child must be protected from 'all forms of physical or mental violence while in the care of parents or others.'[110]

Article 29: The Aims of Education

1. States Parties agree that the education of the child shall be directed to: (a) the development of the child's personality, talents, and mental and physical abilities to their fullest potential; (b) the development of respect for human rights and fundamental freedoms, and for the principles enshrined in the Charter of the United Nations; (c) the development of respect for the child's parents, his or her own cultural identity, language, and values, for the national values of the country in which the child is living, the country from which he or she may originate, and for civilizations different from his or her own; (d) the preparation of the child for responsible life in a free society, in the spirit of understanding, peace, tolerance, equality of sexes, and friendship among all peoples, ethnic, national, and religious groups and persons of indigenous origin; and (e) the development of respect for the natural environment.

The *Handbook* observes that neither the Convention nor the Committee on their comments on the Convention 'details the tools of learning, such as literacy, numeracy, factual knowledge, problem-solving and so forth but addresses learning's basic aims,' which the Committee states are 'to provide the child with life skills, to strengthen the child's capacity to enjoy the full range of human rights and to promote a culture which is infused by appropriate human rights values. The goal is to empower the child by developing his or her skills, learning and other capacities, human dignity, self-esteem and self-confidence.'[III]

The evidence for the effects of participation in the arts is positive. The Culture and Sport Evidence rogramme's 2010 systematic review of the learning impacts for young people authored by the EPPI-Centre (Institute of Education, University of London),[112] shows that, while academic test scores are only minimally improved, there is significant improvement in both cognitive abilities and transferable skills, which, given the Convention's lack of specificity around testable areas such as literacy, numeracy, and factual knowledge and their emphasis on 'empowering the child by developing his or her skills, learning and other capacities, human dignity, self-esteem and self-confidence,'[113] makes participation in arts activities particularly relevant to Article 29.

Mammalian Diving Reflex's intention is not to improve or impart particular skills (we are not interested in increasing the child's chances of becoming a hairstylist, for example) nor teach prescribed ways of evaluating or analyzing their experiences (we are not interested in determining particular ways for critically evaluating a theatre show, for example). Instead, our projects with children are primarily dedicated to demonstrating what the Committee refers to as 'a new social contract';[114] new ways of collaborating with children in the production of life itself, ways that include the child as a rights holder.

This educational aim, then, is directed at the children who participate in our projects, the adults involved with the institutions who engage with us, the general public who encounter our projects in the world, and us, Mammalian Diving Reflex, with the expectation that all parties will benefit from the inclusion of the child, particularly considering, as the Committee states, that it is long-term changes we are looking for in 'political, social, institutional and cultural structures.'[115] These changes will necessarily involve an adjustment in how all affected parties consider themselves and their roles with respect to the child, including the child themself.

This fact is so important that it bears repeating in very simple language: Mammalian Diving Reflex's projects with children are intended to fortify and educate all involved, not just the children.

Within the realm of the child alone, there remains the aim of Article 29 outlined in the Convention, which is strictly to 'empower.' The strategies toward this empowerment are 'by developing his or her skills, learning and other capacities, human dignity, self-esteem and self-confidence,' which we accomplish by attempting to design an environment where all other of the child's rights are utterly respected. If the child becomes adept at styling hair or critically evaluating a theatre show, we regard that as a lovely bonus, but do not position skills-attainment as central to our practice.

Beyond the particulars of what the children will gain through their participation in our projects is a vigilant concern with how they gain what they gain with our dogged dedication to the Committee's first General Comment on the aims of education: ' … education must be provided in a way that respects the inherent dignity of the child and enables the child to express his or her views freely in accordance with Article 12(1). Compliance with the values recognized in Article 29(1) clearly requires that schools (and by extension any institutions that collaborate with children) be child friendly in the fullest sense of the term and that they be consistent in all respects with the dignity of the child.'[116] Again, this, for us, is grounded in the strict adherence to the child's various rights as outlined in the Convention and, concerning these rights in the context of schools or other institutions engaging with children, we are in agreement with the Committee's statement that 'Children do not lose their human rights by virtue of passing through the school gates,' and, as we have outlined in our comments on Article 19, we agree with the Committee's strict limitations on discipline and regard 'punishment which belittles, humiliates, denigrates, scapegoats, threatens, scares or ridicules the child'[117] as violations of their rights to protection from violence and to education.

Article 30: Children of Minorities or Indigenous People

In those States in which ethnic, religious, or linguistic minorities or persons of indigenous origin exist, a child belonging to such a minority or who is indigenous shall not be denied the right, in community with other members of his or her group, to enjoy his or her own culture, to profess and practise his or her own religion, or to use his or her own language.

The *Handbook* states that although a number of the earlier articles cover many of the rights concerning children of minorities or indigenous people, there is still an 'overwhelming evidence of serious and continuing discrimination against minority and indigenous populations [that] justifies mention of their rights in a separate article, to make certain that States pay adequate attention to them.'[118]

With respect to this article, Mammalian Diving Reflex will allow the child to communicate in any language they choose and, while our linguistic capacities are limited, we enjoy the challenge of working with populations who do not speak our language and appreciate the high amount of communication that is actually possible. While we understand the pedagogical imperative of the schools and other institutions to help children to speak the dominant language, Mammalian Diving Reflex's preference is for the child to be comfortable and enjoy their short-term collaboration with us, rather than a strict adherence to policies of appropriate use of particular languages.

Beyond the question of the child's right to the use of a particular language and the enjoyment of a particular culture, Mammalian Diving Reflex is concerned with creating connections across social divides. Most of the cultural organizations we partner with tend to be led, staffed, and their programming dominated by white people, therefore we choose to make every attempt to work with communities – including the communities of children we work with – that are not of the dominant community.

We also note that abundant evidence suggests that, with respect to children's evolving capacities, there are often different expectations when it comes to minority and racialized children, with some children being streamed away from the arts and humanities through a perception of either a lack of aptitude or interest, which researchers have found differs from the students' own views.[119]

We are also sensitive to the representation of different minority groups in popular media, particularly with respect to stereotypes, and we make efforts to showcase children from minority groups, prioritizing them in terms of interviews and photo opportunities. We believe racism and prejudice are not individual problems, isolated within certain intolerant people but, rather, systemic, society-wide attitudes that are reflected and manifested in even the smallest and seemingly most benign choices. When selecting children to feature in interviews in print and on television, we often find that the institutions we partner with stereotype and reinforce inequitable social tendencies by choosing children who have attained a particularly strong and socially reinforced aptitude, articulateness, and cultural fluency. We prefer to invite the children who are not ordinarily offered the opportunity to speak publicly and we do not concern ourselves with the quality of the child's representation of our collaboration, assuring them that we understand that talking to the media is tough, nerve-wracking work and that you only get better by doing.

Article 31: Child's Right to Leisure, Play, and Culture

1. States Parties recognize the right of the child to rest and leisure, to engage in play and recreational activities appropriate to the age of the child, and to participate freely in cultural life and the arts.

2. States Parties shall respect and promote the right of the child to participate fully in cultural and artistic life and shall encourage the provision of appropriate and equal opportunities for cultural, artistic, recreational, and leisure activity.

The *Handbook* states that 'children's right to play is sometimes referred to as the "forgotten right," perhaps because it appears to the adult world as a luxury rather than a necessity of life, and because children always find ways and means of playing, even in the most dire circumstances. But play is an essential part of development: children who are unable to play, for whatever reason, may lack important social and personal skills.'[120] Mammalian recognizes that the right to play is related to the right to freedom of expression and is essential to the artistic process, particularly in the performing arts, and that play and playfulness are central to our artistic practice.

Alarming Trends

In addition, we are in agreement with the International Association for the Child's Right to Play's Declaration of the Child's Right to Play, noting, in particular, a number of 'alarming trends' that are relevant to our practice: 'the over-emphasis on theoretical and academic studies in schools,' the 'increasing commercial exploitation of children and the deterioration of cultural traditions,' and the 'increasing segregation of children in the community.'[121] It is this final trend that our collaborations with children particularly focus on, intending to create moments where children and adults spend time together in play or playful activities.

Primary Vocation

We are also in agreement with the Declaration's statement that 'play is instinctive, voluntary and spontaneous,'[122] and allow these impulses full reign in our projects insofar as they do not threaten health and safety or infringe on the rights of the child or others. We also agree that 'play is a means of learning to live, not a mere passing of time'[123] and therefore can, in many ways, be considered the child's primary vocation, which they enact for the good of the whole society, and we agree that play should be included as a part of all children's environments, including 'institutional settings.'[124]

Health and Safety
Therefore we do not restrict or impede the child's desire to play in any setting whatsoever insofar as they do not threaten health and safety or infringe on the rights of others.

In the event their play disrupt our activities, we respond by informing the children of our feelings and allow them the opportunity to take responsibility for their actions. We do not command the children to stop playing or control any manifestations of physical exuberance.

Again, the previous note on health and safety is relevant: invoking notions of health and safety is a common strategy for controlling and invading the privacy of populations in the case of both adults and children. This is particularly relevant to the children's right to express themselves through play, with declarations of danger used to curtail simple disruption. While the health and safety of all of our collaborators – be they children or adults – is a priority taking precedence above all other, we regard the invocation of health and safety as very serious and consider their arbitrary and opportunistic use, designed to simply control the children for behaviour deemed disruptive, to be a violation of the children's rights of expression and their right to play.

Article 32: Child Labour

1. *States Parties recognize the right of the child to be protected from economic exploitation and from performing any work that is likely to be hazardous or to interfere with the child's education, or to be harmful to the child's health or physical, mental, spiritual, moral, or social development.*
2. *States Parties shall take legislative, administrative, social, and educational measures to ensure the implementation of the present article. To this end, and having regard to the relevant provisions of other international instruments, States Parties shall in particular:*
   (a) provide for a minimum age or minimum ages for admission to employment;
   (b) provide for appropriate regulation of the hours and conditions of employment;
   (c) provide for appropriate penalties or other sanctions to ensure the effective enforcement of the present article.

Article 36: Protection from Other Forms of Exploitation

States Parties shall protect the child against all other forms of exploitation prejudicial to any aspects of the child's welfare.

Mammalian Diving Reflex views Articles 32 and 36 with particular interest because we consider the children artistic collaborators and are wary of exploitation, even if that exploitation is fun yet interferes with their education, for example. The Committee states that States Parties must have regard to the relevant provisions of other international instruments: particularly the International Labour Organization (ILO) Conventions and Recommendations, including in particular the Minimum Age Convention, 1973 (No. 138), which does not apply to work done by children and young persons in schools for general, vocational, or technical education or in other training institutions, or to work done by persons at least 14 years of age in undertakings, 'where such work is carried out in accordance with conditions prescribed by the competent authority.'[125] Article 4 of the 1937 ILO Minimum Age (Non-Industrial Employment) Convention also states that working with children is permitted in 'the interests of art, science or education,' and allow exception from minimum age provisions 'in order to enable children to appear in any public entertainment as long as there are strict safeguards ... for the health, physical development and morals of the children, for ensuring kind treatment of them, adequate rest, and the continuation of their education' and that they do not work beyond midnight.[126] The *Handbook* observes, '[M]any children, in very different national circumstances, carry out work that is entirely consistent with their education and full physical and mental development.'[127]

Relevant to our artistic practice, the *Handbook* identifies 'other forms of exploitation' as including situations 'where children talented in sports, games, performing arts and so forth ... have these talents developed by families, the media, businesses and state authorities at the expense of their overall physical and mental development' and that 'exploitation of young children in the entertainment industry, including television, film, advertising and other modern media, is also a cause for concern.'[128] Though we are a performing arts organization, Mammalian Diving Reflex is dedicated to creating work that does not necessarily develop or exploit particular talents, but instead involves children as they are, attempting to present to the world their exuberance in an unrehearsed and unmitigated way. We are cautious about 'showcasing' the children, preferring, rather, to create a 'performance' out of the children's 'everyday' presence in the world, specifically in venues where they are generally not included, considered, or particularly welcome, demonstrating that their inclusion is actually beneficial to all.

Another form of exploitation we are careful to avoid is that which occurs during research, which many of our projects can be considered; this protocol, for example, can be thought of as the result of 'research' done with children over the years. We are vigilant in gaining the consent of both the parents and children to use any photos and, if a concern is raised, we defer. However, we are also in agreement with the *Handbook* that 'where older children are involved, the issue also relates to their civil rights under the Convention, for example to be heard, to freedom of expression and of association, and to respect their "evolving capacities." It is reasonable to assume that children (are) competent ... to consent to participation in research'[129] and have the capacity to consent to photography. However, we do not disregard the parents' wishes on this matter, regardless of whether or not it is a violation of the child's right.

It is important to point out that recent developments in the world of work and the locations where value is produced have put children at the centre of the work world, often in ways that are not yet acknowledged or, for that matter, fully understood. For example, the very high valuation of online products like Facebook are due to the incredible amounts of labour and time being invested in it by children and young people. Children (and adults) are attracted to Facebook because of the creative presence of their friends, not because of the sophistication of the interface. Without the content provided by the users, Facebook is meaningless. While the content has had other and will have other forms in the past and future – Friendster and Myspace, for example – it is the user-generated content that produces the value, content that is, to a large part, generated by young people and children who are not compensated for their efforts. Sites like YouTube receive millions and millions of hits for videos simply featuring laughing babies and children doing utterly normal things. This is a new frontier for the generation of value, and it's important that children are recognized as important content and, in turn, value providers who remain uncompensated.

Mammalian Diving Reflex notes that exploitation is exploitation regardless of whether the exploited are having a good time while being exploited. It remains that the value of their labour is being captured and utilized by others, and Mammalian Diving Reflex intends to continue to explore the theoretical and practical applications for these insights.

Conclusion

Mammalian Diving Reflex's collaborations with children are not only concerned with the 'preparation of the child for responsible life in a free society,'[130] but, more importantly, for the preparation of society for the free participation of children, the contours of which are not yet visible but will include 'long term changes in political, social, institutional and cultural structures'[131] – in effect, 'a new social contract.'[132] We are in agreement with the handbook that, in matters of education – and we consider our work with children to be related to education – it should not be 'divorced from real-life – a sure path to disaffection, failure and high drop-out rates.'[133] Real life is the focus of our work with children, collaborating with them and the participating adults to generate unusual but real situations where we all encounter new circumstances, people, places, and ideas, while all fully free to be ourselves, unrestricted by the coercive control of others, with full attention paid to the physical and mental health and safety of all and the rights of others.

In truth, the incidents that have motivated the drafting of this protocol are not only completely commonplace, but ridiculously banal: whispering during a performance, ringing a bell without permission, uttering the word *shit*, laughing in public, coughing, running, etc. What all of these minor disturbances have in common is that they triggered an adult to vociferously and angrily shut it down. That such benign actions can trigger such authoritarian impulses speaks to the urgent necessity for a serious consideration of children as rights holders. If these small actions can trigger an adult's anger, think about what many children endure when they actually do transgress, make a mistake, and really piss an adult off. Children – and we were all once children – are the universal victims of unrelenting and ever-present violations of their rights. It truly is non-stop, constant, and ubiquitous. To put it bluntly, children put up with piles of crap that not only should no one have to endure, but that few adults would tolerate for even a millisecond.

We understand that both the Convention and, in turn, this protocol are challenging documents, sometimes even at odds with common sense, but it can't be emphasized enough that the Committee is calling for a 'new social contract,'[134] within which the child's rights will flourish. However, that day has not yet arrived, and we often find ourselves in less than utopian circumstances, having to negotiate multiple and heavily conflicting rights and responsibilities, making a literal and by-the-book application of the Convention and this protocol impossible.

Mammalian Diving Reflex is interested in introducing these ideas and providing forums for attempts at their application, but is keen to accomplish this with abundant communication and generosity, and with the willing consent of all parties. Communication is the key; we want to talk about these ideas, hear where they are challenging, difficult, or currently impossible, and work together with all parties – the children, their parents, their schools, cultural institutions, the State, and the general public – to see how far we can go toward full realization of the rights of children. We do this for the child, but we also do it for those who the child will become: us.

CONVENTION ON THE RIGHTS OF THE CHILD

Adopted and opened for signature, ratification and accession by General Assembly resolution 44/25 of 20 November 1989

Entry into force 2 September 1990, in accordance with Article 49

The States Parties to the present Convention,

Considering that, in accordance with the principles proclaimed in the Charter of the United Nations, recognition of the inherent dignity and of the equal and inalienable rights of all members of the human family is the foundation of freedom, justice and peace in the world,

Bearing in mind that the peoples of the United Nations have, in the Charter, reaffirmed their faith in fundamental human rights and in the dignity and worth of the human person, and have determined to promote social progress and better standards of life in larger freedom,

Recognizing that the United Nations has, in the Universal Declaration of Human Rights and in the International Covenants on Human Rights, proclaimed and agreed that everyone is entitled to all the rights and freedoms set forth therein, without distinction of any kind, such as race, colour, sex, language, religion, political or other opinion, national or social origin, property, birth or other status,

Recalling that, in the Universal Declaration of Human Rights, the United Nations has proclaimed that childhood is entitled to special care and assistance,

Convinced that the family, as the fundamental group of society and the natural environment for the growth and well-being of all its members and particularly children, should be afforded the necessary protection and assistance so that it can fully assume its responsibilities within the community,

Recognizing that the child, for the full and harmonious development of his or her personality, should grow up in a family environment, in an atmosphere of happiness, love and understanding,

Considering that the child should be fully prepared to live an individual life in society, and brought up in the spirit of the ideals proclaimed in the Charter of the United Nations, and in particular in the spirit of peace, dignity, tolerance, freedom, equality and solidarity,

Bearing in mind that the need to extend particular care to the child has been stated in the Geneva Declaration of the Rights of the Child of 1924 and in the Declaration of the Rights of the Child adopted by the General Assembly on 20 November 1959 and recognized in the Universal Declaration of Human Rights, in the International Covenant on Civil and Political Rights (in particular in articles 23 and 24), in the International Covenant on Economic, Social and Cultural Rights (in particular in article 10) and in the statutes and relevant instruments of specialized agencies and international organizations concerned with the welfare of children,

Bearing in mind that, as indicated in the Declaration of the Rights of the Child, 'the child, by reason of his physical and mental immaturity, needs special safeguards and care, including appropriate legal protection, before as well as after birth,'

Recalling the provisions of the Declaration on Social and Legal Principles relating to the Protection and Welfare of Children, with Special Reference to Foster Placement and Adoption Nationally and Internationally; the United Nations Standard Minimum Rules for the Administration of Juvenile Justice (The Beijing Rules); and the Declaration on the Protection of Women and Children in Emergency and Armed Conflict, Recognizing that, in all countries in the world, there are children living in exceptionally difficult conditions, and that such children need special consideration,

Taking due account of the importance of the traditions and cultural values of each people for the protection and harmonious development of the child, Recognizing the importance of international co-operation for improving the living conditions of children in every country, in particular in the developing countries,

Have agreed as follows:

Part I

Article 1
For the purposes of the present Convention, a child means every human being below the age of eighteen years unless under the law applicable to the child, majority is attained earlier.

Article 2
1. States Parties shall respect and ensure the rights set forth in the present Convention to each child within their jurisdiction without discrimination of any kind, irrespective of the child's or his or her parent's or legal guardian's race, colour, sex, language, religion, political or other opinion, national, ethnic or social origin, property, disability, birth or other status.
2. States Parties shall take all appropriate measures to ensure that the child is protected against all forms of discrimination or punishment on the basis of the status, activities, expressed opinions, or beliefs of the child's parents, legal guardians, or family members.

Article 3
1. In all actions concerning children, whether undertaken by public or private social welfare institutions, courts of law, administrative authorities or legislative bodies, the best interests of the child shall be a primary consideration.
2. States Parties undertake to ensure the child such protection and care as is necessary for his or her well-being, taking into account the rights and duties of his or her parents, legal guardians, or other individuals legally responsible for him or her, and, to this end, shall take all appropriate legislative and administrative measures.
3. States Parties shall ensure that the institutions, services and facilities responsible for the care or protection of children shall conform with the standards established by competent authorities, particularly in the areas of safety, health, in the number and suitability of their staff, as well as competent supervision.

Article 4
States Parties shall undertake all appropriate legislative, administrative, and other measures for the implementation of the rights recognized in

the present Convention. With regard to economic, social and cultural rights, States Parties shall undertake such measures to the maximum extent of their available resources and, where needed, within the framework of international co-operation.

Article 5

States Parties shall respect the responsibilities, rights and duties of parents or, where applicable, the members of the extended family or community as provided for by local custom, legal guardians or other persons legally responsible for the child, to provide, in a manner consistent with the evolving capacities of the child, appropriate direction and guidance in the exercise by the child of the rights recognized in the present Convention.

Article 6

1. States Parties recognize that every child has the inherent right to life.
2. States Parties shall ensure to the maximum extent possible the survival and development of the child.

Article 7

1. The child shall be registered immediately after birth and shall have the right from birth to a name, the right to acquire a nationality and, as far as possible, the right to know and be cared for by his or her parents.
2. States Parties shall ensure the implementation of these rights in accordance with their national law and their obligations under the relevant international instruments in this field, in particular where the child would otherwise be stateless.

Article 8

1. States Parties undertake to respect the right of the child to preserve his or her identity, including nationality, name and family relations as recognized by law without unlawful interference.
2. Where a child is illegally deprived of some or all of the elements of his or her identity, States Parties shall provide appropriate assistance and protection, with a view to re-establishing speedily his or her identity.

Article 9

1. States Parties shall ensure that a child shall not be separated from his or her parents against their will, except when competent authorities

subject to judicial review determine, in accordance with applicable law and procedures, that such separation is necessary for the best interests of the child. Such determination may be necessary in a particular case such as one involving abuse or neglect of the child by the parents, or one where the parents are living separately and a decision must be made as to the child's place of residence. 2. In any proceedings pursuant to paragraph 1 of the present article, all interested parties shall be given an opportunity to participate in the proceedings and make their views known.

3. States Parties shall respect the right of the child who is separated from one or both parents to maintain personal relations and direct contact with both parents on a regular basis, except if it is contrary to the child's best interests.

4. Where such separation results from any action initiated by a State Party, such as the detention, imprisonment, exile, deportation or death (including death arising from any cause while the person is in the custody of the State) of one or both parents or of the child, that State Party shall, upon request, provide the parents, the child or, if appropriate, another member of the family with the essential information concerning the whereabouts of the absent member(s) of the family unless the provision of the information would be detrimental to the well-being of the child. States Parties shall further ensure that the submission of such a request shall of itself entail no adverse consequences for the person(s) concerned.

Article 10

1. In accordance with the obligation of States Parties under article 9, paragraph 1, applications by a child or his or her parents to enter or leave a State Party for the purpose of family reunification shall be dealt with by States Parties in a positive, humane and expeditious manner. States Parties shall further ensure that the submission of such a request shall entail no adverse consequences for the applicants and for the members of their family.

2. A child whose parents reside in different States shall have the right to maintain on a regular basis, save in exceptional circumstances, personal relations and direct contacts with both parents. Towards that end and in accordance with the obligation of States Parties under article 9, paragraph 1, States Parties shall respect the right of the child and his or her parents to leave any country, including their own, and to enter their own country. The right to leave any country shall be subject

only to such restrictions as are prescribed by law and which are necessary to protect the national security, public order (ordre public), public health or morals or the rights and freedoms of others and are consistent with the other rights recognized in the present Convention.

Article 11

1. States Parties shall take measures to combat the illicit transfer and non-return of children abroad.
2. To this end, States Parties shall promote the conclusion of bilateral or multilateral agreements or accession to existing agreements.

Article 12

1. States Parties shall assure to the child who is capable of forming his or her own views the right to express those views freely in all matters affecting the child, the views of the child being given due weight in accordance with the age and maturity of the child.
2. For this purpose, the child shall in particular be provided the opportunity to be heard in any judicial and administrative proceedings affecting the child, either directly, or through a representative or an appropriate body, in a manner consistent with the procedural rules of national law.

Article 13

1. The child shall have the right to freedom of expression; this right shall include freedom to seek, receive and impart information and ideas of all kinds, regardless of frontiers, either orally, in writing or in print, in the form of art, or through any other media of the child's choice.
2. The exercise of this right may be subject to certain restrictions, but these shall only be such as are provided by law and are necessary:
(a) For respect of the rights or reputations of others; or (b) For the protection of national security or of public order (ordre public), or of public health or morals.

Article 14

1. States Parties shall respect the right of the child to freedom of thought, conscience and religion.
2. States Parties shall respect the rights and duties of the parents and, when applicable, legal guardians, to provide direction to the child in the exercise of his or her right in a manner consistent with the evolving capacities of the child.

3. Freedom to manifest one's religion or beliefs may be subject only to such limitations as are prescribed by law and are necessary to protect public safety, order, health or morals, or the fundamental rights and freedoms of others.

Article 15
1. States Parties recognize the rights of the child to freedom of association and to freedom of peaceful assembly.
2. No restrictions may be placed on the exercise of these rights other than those imposed in conformity with the law and which are necessary in a democratic society in the interests of national security or public safety, public order (ordre public), the protection of public health or morals or the protection of the rights and freedoms of others.

Article 16
1. No child shall be subjected to arbitrary or unlawful interference with his or her privacy, family, home or correspondence, nor to unlawful attacks on his or her honour and reputation.
2. The child has the right to the protection of the law against such interference or attacks.

Article 17
States Parties recognize the important function performed by the mass media and shall ensure that the child has access to information and material from a diversity of national and international sources, especially those aimed at the promotion of his or her social, spiritual and moral well-being and physical and mental health.

To this end, States Parties shall:

(a) Encourage the mass media to disseminate information and material of social and cultural benefit to the child and in accordance with the spirit of article 29;

(b) Encourage international co-operation in the production, exchange and dissemination of such information and material from a diversity of cultural, national and international sources;

(c) Encourage the production and dissemination of children's books;

(d) Encourage the mass media to have particular regard to the linguistic needs of the child who belongs to a minority group or who is indigenous;

(e) Encourage the development of appropriate guidelines for the protection of the child from information and material injurious to his or her well-being, bearing in mind the provisions of articles 13 and 18.

Article 18

1. States Parties shall use their best efforts to ensure recognition of the principle that both parents have common responsibilities for the upbringing and development of the child. Parents or, as the case may be, legal guardians have the primary responsibility for the upbringing and development of the child. The best interests of the child will be their basic concern.
2. For the purpose of guaranteeing and promoting the rights set forth in the present Convention, States Parties shall render appropriate assistance to parents and legal guardians in the performance of their child-rearing responsibilities and shall ensure the development of institutions, facilities and services for the care of children.
3. States Parties shall take all appropriate measures to ensure that children of working parents have the right to benefit from child-care services and facilities for which they are eligible.

Article 19

1. States Parties shall take all appropriate legislative, administrative, social and educational measures to protect the child from all forms of physical or mental violence, injury or abuse, neglect or negligent treatment, maltreatment or exploitation, including sexual abuse, while in the care of parent(s), legal guardian(s) or any other person who has the care of the child.
2. Such protective measures should, as appropriate, include effective procedures for the establishment of social programmes to provide necessary support for the child and for those who have the care of the child, as well as for other forms of prevention and for identification, reporting, referral, investigation, treatment and follow-up of instances of child maltreatment described heretofore, and, as appropriate, for judicial involvement.

Article 20

1. A child temporarily or permanently deprived of his or her family environment, or in whose own best interests cannot be allowed to remain in that environment, shall be entitled to special protection and assistance provided by the State.
2. States Parties shall in accordance with their national laws ensure alternative care for such a child.
3. Such care could include, inter alia, foster placement, kafalah of Islamic law, adoption or if necessary placement in suitable institutions for

the care of children. When considering solutions, due regard shall be paid to the desirability of continuity in a child's upbringing and to the child's ethnic, religious, cultural and linguistic background.

Article 21

States Parties that recognize and/or permit the system of adoption shall ensure that the best interests of the child shall be the paramount consideration and they shall:

(a) Ensure that the adoption of a child is authorized only by competent authorities who determine, in accordance with applicable law and procedures and on the basis of all pertinent and reliable information, that the adoption is permissible in view of the child's status concerning parents, relatives and legal guardians and that, if required, the persons concerned have given their informed consent to the adoption on the basis of such counselling as may be necessary;

(b) Recognize that inter-country adoption may be considered as an alternative means of child's care, if the child cannot be placed in a foster or an adoptive family or cannot in any suitable manner be cared for in the child's country of origin;

(c) Ensure that the child concerned by inter-country adoption enjoys safeguards and standards equivalent to those existing in the case of national adoption;

(d) Take all appropriate measures to ensure that, in inter-country adoption, the placement does not result in improper financial gain for those involved in it;

(e) Promote, where appropriate, the objectives of the present article by concluding bilateral or multilateral arrangements or agreements, and endeavour, within this framework, to ensure that the placement of the child in another country is carried out by competent authorities or organs.

Article 22

1. States Parties shall take appropriate measures to ensure that a child who is seeking refugee status or who is considered a refugee in accordance with applicable international or domestic law and procedures shall, whether unaccompanied or accompanied by his or her parents or by any other person, receive appropriate protection and humanitarian assistance in the enjoyment of applicable rights set forth in the present Convention and in other international human rights or humanitarian instruments to which the said States are Parties.

2. For this purpose, States Parties shall provide, as they consider appropriate, co-operation in any efforts by the United Nations and other competent intergovernmental organizations or non-governmental organizations co-operating with the United Nations to protect and assist such a child and to trace the parents or other members of the family of any refugee child in order to obtain information necessary for reunification with his or her family. In cases where no parents or other members of the family can be found, the child shall be accorded the same protection as any other child permanently or temporarily deprived of his or her family environment for any reason, as set forth in the present Convention.

Article 23

1. States Parties recognize that a mentally or physically disabled child should enjoy a full and decent life, in conditions which ensure dignity, promote self-reliance and facilitate the child's active participation in the community.

2. States Parties recognize the right of the disabled child to special care and shall encourage and ensure the extension, subject to available resources, to the eligible child and those responsible for his or her care, of assistance for which application is made and which is appropriate to the child's condition and to the circumstances of the parents or others caring for the child.

3. Recognizing the special needs of a disabled child, assistance extended in accordance with paragraph 2 of the present article shall be provided free of charge, whenever possible, taking into account the financial resources of the parents or others caring for the child, and shall be designed to ensure that the disabled child has effective access to and receives education, training, health care services, rehabilitation services, preparation for employment and recreation opportunities in a manner conducive to the child's achieving the fullest possible social integration and individual development, including his or her cultural and spiritual development.

4. States Parties shall promote, in the spirit of international cooperation, the exchange of appropriate information in the field of preventive health care and of medical, psychological and functional treatment of disabled children, including dissemination of and access to information concerning methods of rehabilitation, education and vocational services, with the aim of enabling States Parties to improve their capabilities and skills and to widen their experience in these areas. In this regard, particular account shall be taken of the needs of developing countries.

Article 24

1. States Parties recognize the right of the child to the enjoyment of the highest attainable standard of health and to facilities for the treatment of illness and rehabilitation of health. States Parties shall strive to ensure that no child is deprived of his or her right of access to such health care services.

2. States Parties shall pursue full implementation of this right and, in particular, shall take appropriate measures:

(a) To diminish infant and child mortality;

(b) To ensure the provision of necessary medical assistance and health care to all children with emphasis on the development of primary health care;

(c) To combat disease and malnutrition, including within the framework of primary health care, through, inter alia, the application of readily available technology and through the provision of adequate nutritious foods and clean drinking-water, taking into consideration the dangers and risks of environmental pollution;

(d) To ensure appropriate pre-natal and post-natal health care for mothers;

(e) To ensure that all segments of society, in particular parents and children, are informed, have access to education and are supported in the use of basic knowledge of child health and nutrition, the advantages of breastfeeding, hygiene and environmental sanitation and the prevention of accidents;

(f) To develop preventive health care, guidance for parents and family planning education and services.

3. States Parties shall take all effective and appropriate measures with a view to abolishing traditional practices prejudicial to the health of children.

4. States Parties undertake to promote and encourage international co-operation with a view to achieving progressively the full realization of the right recognized in the present article. In this regard, particular account shall be taken of the needs of developing countries.

Article 25

States Parties recognize the right of a child who has been placed by the competent authorities for the purposes of care, protection or treatment of his or her physical or mental health, to a periodic review of the treatment provided to the child and all other circumstances relevant to his or her placement.

Article 26

1. States Parties shall recognize for every child the right to benefit from social security, including social insurance, and shall take the necessary measures to achieve the full realization of this right in accordance with their national law.

2. The benefits should, where appropriate, be granted, taking into account the resources and the circumstances of the child and persons having responsibility for the maintenance of the child, as well as any other consideration relevant to an application for benefits made by or on behalf of the child.

Article 27

1. States Parties recognize the right of every child to a standard of living adequate for the child's physical, mental, spiritual, moral and social development.

2. The parent(s) or others responsible for the child have the primary responsibility to secure, within their abilities and financial capacities, the conditions of living necessary for the child's development.

3. States Parties, in accordance with national conditions and within their means, shall take appropriate measures to assist parents and others responsible for the child to implement this right and shall in case of need provide material assistance and support programmes, particularly with regard to nutrition, clothing and housing.

4. States Parties shall take all appropriate measures to secure the recovery of maintenance for the child from the parents or other persons having financial responsibility for the child, both within the State Party and from abroad. In particular, where the person having financial responsibility for the child lives in a State different from that of the child, States Parties shall promote the accession to international agreements or the conclusion of such agreements, as well as the making of other appropriate arrangements.

Article 28

1. States Parties recognize the right of the child to education, and with a view to achieving this right progressively and on the basis of equal opportunity, they shall, in particular:

(a) Make primary education compulsory and available free to all;

(b) Encourage the development of different forms of secondary education, including general and vocational education, make them available and accessible to every child, and take appropriate measures such as the introduction of free education and offering financial assistance in case of need;

(c) Make higher education accessible to all on the basis of capacity by every appropriate means;

(d) Make educational and vocational information and guidance available and accessible to all children;

(e) Take measures to encourage regular attendance at schools and the reduction of drop-out rates.

2. States Parties shall take all appropriate measures to ensure that school discipline is administered in a manner consistent with the child's human dignity and in conformity with the present Convention.

3. States Parties shall promote and encourage international cooperation in matters relating to education, in particular with a view to contributing to the elimination of ignorance and illiteracy throughout the world and facilitating access to scientific and technical knowledge and modern teaching methods. In this regard, particular account shall be taken of the needs of developing countries.

Article 29

1. States Parties agree that the education of the child shall be directed to:

(a) The development of the child's personality, talents and mental and physical abilities to their fullest potential;

(b) The development of respect for human rights and fundamental freedoms, and for the principles enshrined in the Charter of the United Nations;

(c) The development of respect for the child's parents, his or her own cultural identity, language and values, for the national values of the country in which the child is living, the country from which he or she may originate, and for civilizations different from his or her own;

(d) The preparation of the child for responsible life in a free society, in the spirit of understanding, peace, tolerance, equality of sexes, and friendship among all peoples, ethnic, national and religious groups and persons of indigenous origin;

(e) The development of respect for the natural environment.

2. No part of the present article or article 28 shall be construed so as to interfere with the liberty of individuals and bodies to establish and direct educational institutions, subject always to the observance of the principle set forth in paragraph 1 of the present article and to the requirements that the education given in such institutions shall conform to such minimum standards as may be laid down by the State.

Article 30

In those States in which ethnic, religious or linguistic minorities or persons of indigenous origin exist, a child belonging to such a minority or who is indigenous shall not be denied the right, in community with other members of his or her group, to enjoy his or her own culture, to profess and practise his or her own religion, or to use his or her own language.

Article 31

1. States Parties recognize the right of the child to rest and leisure, to engage in play and recreational activities appropriate to the age of the child and to participate freely in cultural life and the arts.
2. States Parties shall respect and promote the right of the child to participate fully in cultural and artistic life and shall encourage the provision of appropriate and equal opportunities for cultural, artistic, recreational and leisure activity.

Article 32

1. States Parties recognize the right of the child to be protected from economic exploitation and from performing any work that is likely to be hazardous or to interfere with the child's education, or to be harmful to the child's health or physical, mental, spiritual, moral or social development.
2. States Parties shall take legislative, administrative, social and educational measures to ensure the implementation of the present article. To this end, and having regard to the relevant provisions of other international instruments, States Parties shall in particular:
(a) Provide for a minimum age or minimum ages for admission to employment;
(b) Provide for appropriate regulation of the hours and conditions of employment;
(c) Provide for appropriate penalties or other sanctions to ensure the effective enforcement of the present article.

Article 33
States Parties shall take all appropriate measures, including legislative, administrative, social and educational measures, to protect children from the illicit use of narcotic drugs and psychotropic substances as defined in the relevant international treaties, and to prevent the use of children in the illicit production and trafficking of such substances.

Article 34
States Parties undertake to protect the child from all forms of sexual exploitation and sexual abuse. For these purposes, States Parties shall in particular take all appropriate national, bilateral and multilateral measures to prevent:
(a) The inducement or coercion of a child to engage in any unlawful sexual activity;
(b) The exploitative use of children in prostitution or other unlawful sexual practices;
(c) The exploitative use of children in pornographic performances and materials.

Article 35
States Parties shall take all appropriate national, bilateral and multilateral measures to prevent the abduction of, the sale of or traffic in children for any purpose or in any form.

Article 36
States Parties shall protect the child against all other forms of exploitation prejudicial to any aspects of the child's welfare.

Article 37
States Parties shall ensure that:
(a) No child shall be subjected to torture or other cruel, inhuman or degrading treatment or punishment. Neither capital punishment nor life imprisonment without possibility of release shall be imposed for offences committed by persons below eighteen years of age;
(b) No child shall be deprived of his or her liberty unlawfully or arbitrarily. The arrest, detention or imprisonment of a child shall be in conformity with the law and shall be used only as a measure of last resort and for the shortest appropriate period of time;
(c) Every child deprived of liberty shall be treated with humanity and respect for the inherent dignity of the human person, and in a manner

which takes into account the needs of persons of his or her age. In particular, every child deprived of liberty shall be separated from adults unless it is considered in the child's best interest not to do so and shall have the right to maintain contact with his or her family through correspondence and visits, save in exceptional circumstances; (d) Every child deprived of his or her liberty shall have the right to prompt access to legal and other appropriate assistance, as well as the right to challenge the legality of the deprivation of his or her liberty before a court or other competent, independent and impartial authority, and to a prompt decision on any such action.

Article 38

1. States Parties undertake to respect and to ensure respect for rules of international humanitarian law applicable to them in armed conflicts which are relevant to the child.
2. States Parties shall take all feasible measures to ensure that persons who have not attained the age of fifteen years do not take a direct part in hostilities.
3. States Parties shall refrain from recruiting any person who has not attained the age of fifteen years into their armed forces. In recruiting among those persons who have attained the age of fifteen years but who have not attained the age of eighteen years, States Parties shall endeavour to give priority to those who are oldest.
4. In accordance with their obligations under international humanitarian law to protect the civilian population in armed conflicts, States Parties shall take all feasible measures to ensure protection and care of children who are affected by an armed conflict.

Article 39

States Parties shall take all appropriate measures to promote physical and psychological recovery and social reintegration of a child victim of: any form of neglect, exploitation, or abuse; torture or any other form of cruel, inhuman or degrading treatment or punishment; or armed conflicts. Such recovery and reintegration shall take place in an environment which fosters the health, self-respect and dignity of the child.

Article 40

1. States Parties recognize the right of every child alleged as, accused of, or recognized as having infringed the penal law to be treated in a manner consistent with the promotion of the child's sense of dignity

and worth, which reinforces the child's respect for the human rights and fundamental freedoms of others and which takes into account the child's age and the desirability of promoting the child's reintegration and the child's assuming a constructive role in society.

2. To this end, and having regard to the relevant provisions of international instruments, States Parties shall, in particular, ensure that:

(a) No child shall be alleged as, be accused of, or recognized as having infringed the penal law by reason of acts or omissions that were not prohibited by national or international law at the time they were committed;

(b) Every child alleged as or accused of having infringed the penal law has at least the following guarantees:

(i) To be presumed innocent until proven guilty according to law;

(ii) To be informed promptly and directly of the charges against him or her, and, if appropriate, through his or her parents or legal guardians, and to have legal or other appropriate assistance in the preparation and presentation of his or her defence;

(iii) To have the matter determined without delay by a competent, independent and impartial authority or judicial body in a fair hearing according to law, in the presence of legal or other appropriate assistance and, unless it is considered not to be in the best interest of the child, in particular, taking into account his or her age or situation, his or her parents or legal guardians;

(iv) Not to be compelled to give testimony or to confess guilt; to examine or have examined adverse witnesses and to obtain the participation and examination of witnesses on his or her behalf under conditions of equality;

(v) If considered to have infringed the penal law, to have this decision and any measures imposed in consequence thereof reviewed by a higher competent, independent and impartial authority or judicial body according to law;

(vi) To have the free assistance of an interpreter if the child cannot understand or speak the language used;

(vii) To have his or her privacy fully respected at all stages of the proceedings.

3. States Parties shall seek to promote the establishment of laws, procedures, authorities and institutions specifically applicable to children alleged as, accused of, or recognized as having infringed the penal law, and, in particular:

(a) The establishment of a minimum age below which children shall be presumed not to have the capacity to infringe the penal law;

(b) Whenever appropriate and desirable, measures for dealing with such children without resorting to judicial proceedings, providing that human rights and legal safeguards are fully respected.

4. A variety of dispositions, such as care, guidance and supervision orders; counselling; probation; foster care; education and vocational training programmes and other alternatives to institutional care shall be available to ensure that children are dealt with in a manner appropriate to their well-being and proportionate both to their circumstances and the offence.

Article 41

Nothing in the present Convention shall affect any provisions which are more conducive to the realization of the rights of the child and which may be contained in:

(a) The law of a State party; or

(b) International law in force for that State.

Part II

Article 42

States Parties undertake to make the principles and provisions of the Convention widely known, by appropriate and active means, to adults and children alike.

Article 43

1. For the purpose of examining the progress made by States Parties in achieving the realization of the obligations undertaken in the present Convention, there shall be established a Committee on the Rights of the Child, which shall carry out the functions hereinafter provided.

2. The Committee shall consist of eighteen experts of high moral standing and recognized competence in the field covered by this Convention.* The members of the Committee shall be elected by States Parties from among their nationals and shall serve in their personal capacity, consideration being given to equitable geographical distribution, as well as to the principal legal systems.

3. The members of the Committee shall be elected by secret ballot from a list of persons nominated by States Parties. Each State Party may nominate one person from among its own nationals.

4. The initial election to the Committee shall be held no later than six months after the date of the entry into force of the present Convention and thereafter every second year. At least four months before the date of each election, the Secretary-General of the United Nations shall address a letter to States Parties inviting them to submit their nominations within two months. The Secretary-General shall subsequently prepare a list in alphabetical order of all persons thus nominated, indicating States Parties which have nominated them, and shall submit it to the States Parties to the present Convention.

5. The elections shall be held at meetings of States Parties convened by the Secretary-General at United Nations Headquarters. At those meetings, for which two-thirds of States Parties shall constitute a quorum, the persons elected to the Committee shall be those who obtain the largest number of votes and an absolute majority of the votes of the representatives of States Parties present and voting.

6. The members of the Committee shall be elected for a term of four years. They shall be eligible for re-election if renominated. The term of five of the members elected at the first election shall expire at the end of two years; immediately after the first election, the names of these five members shall be chosen by lot by the Chairman of the meeting.

7. If a member of the Committee dies or resigns or declares that for any other cause he or she can no longer perform the duties of the Committee, the State Party which nominated the member shall appoint another expert from among its nationals to serve for the remainder of the term, subject to the approval of the Committee.

8. The Committee shall establish its own rules of procedure.

9. The Committee shall elect its officers for a period of two years.

10. The meetings of the Committee shall normally be held at United Nations Headquarters or at any other convenient place as determined by the Committee. The Committee shall normally meet annually. The duration of the meetings of the Committee shall be determined, and reviewed, if necessary, by a meeting of the States Parties to the present Convention, subject to the approval of the General Assembly.

11. The Secretary-General of the United Nations shall provide the necessary staff and facilities for the effective performance of the functions of the Committee under the present Convention.

12. With the approval of the General Assembly, the members of the Committee established under the present Convention shall receive emoluments from United Nations resources on such terms and conditions as the Assembly may decide.

Article 44

1. States Parties undertake to submit to the Committee, through the Secretary-General of the United Nations, reports on the measures they have adopted which give effect to the rights recognized herein and on the progress made on the enjoyment of those rights
(a) Within two years of the entry into force of the Convention for the State Party concerned;
(b) Thereafter every five years.

2. Reports made under the present article shall indicate factors and difficulties, if any, affecting the degree of fulfilment of the obligations under the present Convention. Reports shall also contain sufficient information to provide the Committee with a comprehensive understanding of the implementation of the Convention in the country concerned.

3. A State Party which has submitted a comprehensive initial report to the Committee need not, in its subsequent reports submitted in accordance with paragraph 1 (b) of the present article, repeat basic information previously provided.

4. The Committee may request from States Parties further information relevant to the implementation of the Convention.

5. The Committee shall submit to the General Assembly, through the Economic and Social Council, every two years, reports on its activities.

6. States Parties shall make their reports widely available to the public in their own countries.

Article 45

In order to foster the effective implementation of the Convention and to encourage international co-operation in the field covered by the Convention:

(a) The specialized agencies, the United Nations Children's Fund, and other United Nations organs shall be entitled to be represented at the consideration of the implementation of such provisions of the present Convention as fall within the scope of their mandate. The Committee may invite the specialized agencies, the United Nations Children's Fund and other competent bodies as it may consider appropriate to provide expert advice on the implementation of the Convention in areas falling within the scope of their respective mandates. The Committee may invite the specialized agencies, the United Nations Children's Fund, and other United Nations organs to submit reports on the implementation of the Convention in areas falling within the scope of their activities;

(b) The Committee shall transmit, as it may consider appropriate, to the specialized agencies, the United Nations Children's Fund and other competent bodies, any reports from States Parties that contain a request, or indicate a need, for technical advice or assistance, along with the Committee's observations and suggestions, if any, on these requests or indications;

(c) The Committee may recommend to the General Assembly to request the Secretary-General to undertake on its behalf studies on specific issues relating to the rights of the child;

(d) The Committee may make suggestions and general recommendations based on information received pursuant to articles 44 and 45 of the present Convention. Such suggestions and general recommendations shall be transmitted to any State Party concerned and reported to the General Assembly, together with comments, if any, from States Parties.

Part III

Article 46

The present Convention shall be open for signature by all States.

Article 47

The present Convention is subject to ratification. Instruments of ratification shall be deposited with the Secretary-General of the United Nations.

Article 48

The present Convention shall remain open for accession by any State. The instruments of accession shall be deposited with the Secretary-General of the United Nations.

Article 49

1. The present Convention shall enter into force on the thirtieth day following the date of deposit with the Secretary-General of the United Nations of the twentieth instrument of ratification or accession.
2. For each State ratifying or acceding to the Convention after the deposit of the twentieth instrument of ratification or accession, the Convention shall enter into force on the thirtieth day after the deposit by such State of its instrument of ratification or accession.

Article 50

1. Any State Party may propose an amendment and file it with the Secretary-General of the United Nations. The Secretary-General shall thereupon communicate the proposed amendment to States Parties, with a request that they indicate whether they favour a conference of States Parties for the purpose of considering and voting upon the proposals. In the event that, within four months from the date of such communication, at least one third of the States Parties favour such a conference, the Secretary-General shall convene the conference under the auspices of the United Nations. Any amendment adopted by a majority of States Parties present and voting at the conference shall be submitted to the General Assembly for approval.

2. An amendment adopted in accordance with paragraph 1 of the present article shall enter into force when it has been approved by the General Assembly of the United Nations and accepted by a two-thirds majority of States Parties.

3. When an amendment enters into force, it shall be binding on those States Parties which have accepted it, other States Parties still being bound by the provisions of the present Convention and any earlier amendments which they have accepted.

Article 51

1. The Secretary-General of the United Nations shall receive and circulate to all States the text of reservations made by States at the time of ratification or accession.

2. A reservation incompatible with the object and purpose of the present Convention shall not be permitted.

3. Reservations may be withdrawn at any time by notification to that effect addressed to the Secretary-General of the United Nations, who shall then inform all States. Such notification shall take effect on the date on which it is received by the Secretary-General.

Article 52

A State Party may denounce the present Convention by written notification to the Secretary-General of the United Nations. Denunciation becomes effective one year after the date of receipt of the notification by the Secretary-General.

Article 53
The Secretary-General of the United Nations is designated as the depositary of the present Convention.

Article 54
The original of the present Convention, of which the Arabic, Chinese, English, French, Russian and Spanish texts are equally authentic, shall be deposited with the Secretary-General of the United Nations. In witness thereof the undersigned plenipotentiaries, being duly authorized thereto by their respective Governments, have signed the present Convention.

The General Assembly, in its resolution 50/155 of 21 December 1995, approved the amendment to article 43, paragraph 2, of the Convention on the Rights of the Child, replacing the word "ten" with the word "eighteen." The amendment entered into force on 18 November 2002 when it had been accepted by a two-thirds majority of the States parties (128 out of 191).

THE INTERNATIONAL PLAY ASSOCIATION'S DECLARATION OF THE CHILD'S RIGHT TO PLAY

The IPA Declaration of the Child's Right to Play was produced in November 1977 at the IPA Malta Consultation held in preparation for the International Year of the Child (1979). It was revised by the IPA International Council in Vienna, September 1982, and in Barcelona, September 1989. It should be read in conjunction with Article 31 of the U.N. Convention on the Rights of the Child (adopted by the General Assembly of the U.N., November 20, 1989), which states that the child has a right to leisure, play, and participation in cultural and artistic activities.

What Is Play?

CHILDREN are the foundation of the world's future.

CHILDREN have played at all times throughout history and in all cultures.

PLAY, along with the basic needs of nutrition, health, shelter and education, is vital to develop the potential of all children.

PLAY is communication and expression, combining thought and action; it gives satisfaction and a feeling of achievement.

PLAY is instinctive, voluntary, and spontaneous.

PLAY is a means of learning to live, not a mere passing of time.

Alarming Trends Affecting Childhood

IPA is deeply concerned by a number of alarming trends and their negative impact on children's development.

- Society's indifference to the importance of play
- Overemphasis on theoretical and academic studies in schools.
- Increasing numbers of children living with inadequate provisions for survival and development.
- Inadequate environmental planning, which results in a lack of basic amenities, inappropriate housing forms, and poor traffic management.
- Increasing commercial exploitation of children and the deterioration of cultural traditions.
- Lack of access for third world women to basic training in childcare and development.
- Inadequate preparation of children to cope with life in a rapidly changing society.

- Increasing segregation of children in the community.
- The increasing numbers of working children, and their unacceptable working conditions.
- Constant exposure of children to war, violence, exploitation, and destruction.
- Overemphasis on unhealthy competition and 'winning at all costs' in children's sports.

Proposals for Action

The following proposals are listed under the names of government departments having a measure of responsibility for children.

Health

Play is essential for the physical and mental health of the child.
- Establish programmes for professionals and parents about the benefits of play from birth onwards.
- Ensure basic conditions (nutrition, sanitation, clean water and air) which promote the healthy survival and development of all children.
- Incorporate play into community programmes designed to maintain children's physical and mental health.
- Include play as an integral part of all children's environments, including hospitals and other institutional settings.

Education

Play is part of education.
- Provide opportunities for initiatives, interaction, creativity, and socialization through play in formal education systems.
- Include studies of the importance of play and the means of play provision in the training of all professionals and volunteers working with and for children.
- Strengthen play provision in primary schools to enhance learning and to maintain attendance and motivation.
- Reduce the incompatibilities between daily life, work, and education by involving schools and colleges, and by using public buildings for community play programs.
- Ensure that working children have access to play and learning opportunities outside of the system of formal education.

Welfare

Play is an essential part of family and community life.

- Ensure that play is accepted as an integral part of social development and social care.
- Promote measures that strengthen positive relationships between parents and children.
- Ensure that play is part of community-based services designed to integrate children with physical, mental or emotional disabilities into the community.
- Provide safe play environments that protect children against abduction, sexual abuse, and physical violence.

Leisure

Children need opportunities to play at leisure.

- Provide time, space, materials, natural settings, and programmes with leaders where children may develop a sense of belonging, self-esteem, and enjoyment through play.
- Enable interaction between children and people of all backgrounds and ages in leisure settings.
- Encourage the conservation and use of traditional indigenous games.
- Stop the commercial exploitation of children's play, and the production and sale of war toys and games of violence and destruction.
- Promote the use of co-operative games and fair play for children in sports.
- Provide all children, particularly those with special needs, with access to a diversity of play environments, toys, and play materials through community programmes such as pre-school play groups, toy libraries, and play buses.

Planning

The needs of the child must have priority in the planning of human settlements.

- Ensure that children and young people can participate in making decisions that affect their surroundings and their access to them. When planning new or reorganizing existing developments, recognise the child's small size and limited range of activity.
- Disseminate existing knowledge about play facilities and play programmes to planning professionals and politicians.
- Oppose the building of high-rise housing and provide opportunities to mitigate its detrimental effects on children and families.

- Enable children to move easily about the community by providing safe pedestrian access through urban neighbourhoods, better traffic management, and improved public transportation.
- Increase awareness of the high vulnerability of children living in slum settlements, tenements, and derelict neighbourhoods.
- Reserve adequate and appropriate space for play and recreation through statutory provision.

Affirmation

IPA is determined to sustain the momentum created by the International Year of the Child in 1979 to arouse world opinion for the improvement of the life of children, and;

AFFIRMS its belief in the United Nations' Declaration of the Rights of the Child, which in Article 7 states 'The child shall have full opportunity to play and recreation, which should be directed to the same purposes as education; society and the public authorities shall endeavour to promote the enjoyment of this right'; and endorses its belief in Article 31 of the Convention on the Rights of the Child.

RECOGNISES that the population of children in developing countries is three-quarters of the world's total child population, and that efforts directed at the promotion of education and literacy, and the stopping of environmental deprivation, would improve the capacities of the poorest.

AFFIRMS its commitment to working with other national and international organisations to ensure basic conditions of survival for all children in order that they may fully develop as human beings.

ACKNOWLEDGES that each country is responsible for preparing its own courses of public and political action in the light of its culture, climate and social, political, and economic structure;

RECOGNISES that the full participation of the community is essential in planning and developing programmes and services to meet the needs, wishes, and aspirations of children.

ASSURES its co-operation with UN agencies and other international and national organizations involved with children.

APPEALS to all countries and organizations to take action to counteract the alarming trends which jeopardise children's healthy development and to give high priority to long-term programmes designed to ensure for all time: THE CHILD'S RIGHT TO PLAY.

Notes

1. Mona Pare, 'Inclusion and Participation in Special Education Processes in Ontario, Canada,' in *International Perspective and Empirical Findings on Child Participation*, ed. Tali Gal (Oxford: Oxford University Press, 2015), 51-73.

2. The United Nations Committee on the Rights of the Child, 'Report on the forty-third session, Day of General Discussion on the Right to be Heard, Recommendations, Preamble' (Geneva: The United Nations, 2006).

3. Thomas Piketty, *Capital in the Twenty-First Century*. (New York: Harvard University Press, 2014).

4. Judith Butler, *Notes Toward a Performative Theory of Assembly* (Cambridge, MA: Harvard University Press, 2015).

5. Alison M. Watson, *The Child in International Politics: A Place at the Table* (London: Routledge, 2009).

6. Martha Albertson Fineman, 'The Vulnerable Subject: Anchoring Equality in the Human Condition,' *Yale Journal of Law and Feminism* 20, no. 1, article 2 (2008).

7. *Cambridge Journal of Regions, Economy and Society* (vol. 6, issue 1, 2013), *Creatives after the Crash*, features a number of articles presenting evidence that the creative industries managed to survive the market crash of 2008 better than many other industries.

8. booba1234, *David After Dentist*, Youtube video, 1:28 (January 30, 2009). youtu.be/txqiwrbYGrs; www.davidafterdentist.com/.

9. Allen J. Scott, 'Creative Cities: Conceptual Issues and Policy Questions,' *Journal of Urban Affairs* 28, no. 1 (2006): 15.

10. O'Brien's video can be viewed on the *New York Times* website: nyti.ms/2ny6cDe.

11. Nicolas Bourriaud, *Relational Aesthetics*, trans. Simon Pleasance and Fronza Woods (Dijon: Les Presses du Réel, 1998): 74

12. Ibid., 14.

13. Anne Wihstutz, 'The Significance of Care and Domestic Work to Children: A German Portrayal,' in *Working to Be Someone: Child Focused Research and Practice with Working Children*, ed. Beatrice Hungerland, Manfred Liebel, Brian Milne, and Anne Wihstutz (London: Jessica Kingsley Publishers, 2007): 77-86.

14. Jeylan T. Mortimer, 'Working and Growing Up in America: Myths and Realities,' in *Working to Be Someone*: 117-122.

15. Madeleine Leonard, 'Child Employment in Northern Ireland: Myths and Realities,' in *Working to Be Someone*: 145-150.

16. Nicholas Ridout, 'Performance in the Service Economy: Outsourcing and Delegation,' in *Double Agent*, ed. Claire Bishop and Silvia Tramontana (London: Institute of Contemporary Arts, 2009): 136-131.

17. 'What Is Child Labour.' International Labour Organization. Accessed July 12, 2017. www.ilo.org/ipec/facts/lang--en/index.htm.

18. Stephen J. Ceci and Wendy M. Williams, 'Schooling, Intelligence and Income,' *American Psychologist* 52, no. 10 (1997): 1051-1058. Michael T. French, Jenny F. Homer, Ioana Popovici, and Philip K. Robins, 'What You Do in High School Matters: High School GPA, Educational Attainment, and Labor Market Earnings as a Young Adult,' *Eastern Economic Journal* 4, no. 3 (2015): 370-386.

19. The Children and Young Persons Act can be found at www.legislation.gov.uk/ukpga/1963/37/section/37.

20. Wihstutz, 'The Significance of Care': 77-86.

21. David Oldman, 'Childhood as a Mode of Production,' in *Children's Childhoods, Observed and Experienced*, ed. Barry Mayall (London: Palmer Press, 1994): 155.

22. Ibid.

23. Jens Qvortup, 'School-work, paid work and the changing obligations of childhood,' in *Future of Childhood: Hidden Hand: International Perspectives on Children's Work and Labour*, ed. Angela Bolton, Phillip Mizen, and Christopher Pole (Abingdon, Oxon, U.S.: Routledge, 2001): 91-107.

24. Ibid., 93, 94.

25. Peter Gray, 'The Decline of Play and the Rise of Psychopathology in Children and Adolescents,' *American Journal of Play* 3, no. 4 (2011): 443-463.

26. Dieter Kirchofer, 'The Reintegration of Children into the Adult World of Work: Ominous Sign or Cause for Optimism?' in *Working to Be Someone*: 43-54.

27. Luc Boltanski, and Ève Chiapello, *The New Spirit of Capitalism*, trans. Gregory Elliot (London, New York: Verso, 2007): 190.

28. Stuart Brown and Christopher Vaughan, *Play: How It Shapes the Brain, Opens the Imagination, and Invigorates the Soul* (London: Penguin Books, 2009).

29. In Jared Keller, 'The Psychological Case for Adult Play,' *Pacific Standard*, April 9, 2015. psmag.com/social-justice/throw-out-your-computer-and-grab-some-legos.

30. Benjamin Kipps, *How to Tie a Bow Tie for Dummies*, Youtube video, 6:06 (May 13, 2012). youtu.be/ZoeNCvGbfYM. Ben is not a mega-YouTube celebrity, but just a kid with 211 followers and six videos: two of him playing his clarinet at home; a cover of the Plain White T's 'Hey There, Delilah,' with Ben on the guitar; Ben decisively losing to a Carolina Reaper (one of the hottest peppers in the world); and his masterpiece, *How to Tie a Bow Tie for Dummies*, the only one of his videos racking in over 500 views, with 152,337 in July 2017.

31. Newzoo. 'Top 100 Countries by Game Revenues,' Newzoo, June 2017. Accessed July 16, 2017. newzoo.com/insights/rankings/top-100-countries-by-game-revenues/.

32. Sophie Densham, 'UK Game Market Soars Past £4.1 Billion,' Association for UK Interactive Entertainment, February 11, 2016. Accessed July 16, 2017. ukie.org.uk/node/29702.

33. Jeff Schmidt, *Disciplined Minds: A Critical Look at Salaried Professionals and the Soul-battering System That Shapes Their Lives* (Lanham, MD: Rowman & Littlefield Publishers, 2001).

34. Darren O'Donnell, *Social Acupuncture* (Toronto: Coach House Books, 2006).

35. Sack, Sally. Foreword to *What Is Art? Conversation with Joseph Beuys*, ed. Volker Harlan (Forest Row: Clairview, 2012).

36. Andy Curtis, *HyperNormalisation*, dir. Andy Curtis (London: BBC, 2016). www.bbc.co.uk/programmes/p04b183c.

37. Zak Cheney Rice, 'A Black Man Playing "Pokemon Go" Was Surrounded by Iowa City Officers with Guns Aimed at Him,' *Business Insider*, July 25, 2016. Accessed July 17, 2017. www.businessinsider.com/black-playing-pokemon-gochased-by-police-2016-7?IR=T.

38. Robin Wright, Lindsay John, and Julia Sheel, 'Lessons Learned from the National Arts and Youth Demonstration Project,' *Journal of Children and Family Studies*, vol. 16, no. 1 (2007): 48-58.

39. Ben Durbin et al., *The Impact of Creative Partnerships on School Attainment and Attendance* (Slough: National Foundation for Educational Research, 2010). Accessed July 17, 2012.

www.creativitycultureeducation.org/wp-content/uploads/nfer-2010-impact-of-
creative-partnerships-on-young-peoples-behavior-and-attainment-234.pdf.

40. Realist social theory looks for regularities that are somewhat dependable – demi-
regularities, as they are called among the realist camp. These are findings that can be
said to tend to happen, but not always. The complexity of the social world makes it
impossible to nail down causality to completely consistent reproducibility, and the
realist accepts this frustrating fact, looking for broader patterns that can be said to
hold more or less true across a number of situations. Realist social theory is the theory
we look to when developing policy; it's workaday theory, by no means a grand theory.
But it's a theory we use when we actually want to get things done.

41. Ray Pawson, *The Science of Evaluation: A Realist Manifesto* (London: Sage Publications,
2013).

42. Hill Strategies Research, *Mapping Artists and Cultural Working in Canada's Largest Cities*
(Hamilton: Hill Strategies Research), February 9. 2010. Accessed July 17, 2017. www.hill-
strategies.com/content/mapping-artists-and-cultural-workers-canada%E2%80%99s-
large-cities2010.

43. Sharon Zukin, 'Gentrification: Culture and Capital in the Urban Core,' *Annual Review of
Sociology* (1987): 132, 129-137.

44. Cameron Stuart and Jon Coaffee, 'Art, Gentrification and Regeneration: From Artist as
Pioneer to Public Arts,' *European Journal of Housing Policy* 5, no. 1 (2005): 39-58

45. Katie M. Mazer, Katharine N. Rankin, 'The Social Space of Gentrification: The Politics
of Neighbourhood Accessibility in Toronto's Downtown West,' *Environment and Planning D: Society and Space* 29, 5 (2011): 822.

46. Tim Butler and Garry Robson, 'Social Capital, Gentrification and Neighbourhood
Change in London: A Comparison of Three South London Neighbourhoods,' *Urban
Studies* 38, 12 (2001): 2157.

47. Bob Ramsay, 'Toronto Arts Boards in Dire Need of Diversity,' *Toronto Star*, June 10,
2015. Accessed July 19, 2017. www.thestar.com/opinion/commentary/2015/06/10/
toronto-arts-boards-in-dire-need-of-diversity.html.

48. The Warwick Commission, *Enriching Britain: Culture, Creativity and Growth: The 2015
Report by the Warwick Commission on the Future of Cultural Value* (Coventry: University
of Warwick, 2015). Accessed July 19, 2017. www2.warwick.ac.uk/research/warwickcom-
mission/futureculture/finalreport/.

49. Roberto Bedoya, 'Considering Whiteness,' Engaging Matters (blog), *Arts Journal*, February 20 , 2016 (accessed July 19 , 2017 ; www.artsjournal.com/engage/2013/02/
considering-whiteness); Mike Boehm, 'Study Sends "Wake-up Call" about Black and
Latino Arts Groups' meager funding,' *Los Angeles Times*, October 12, 2015 (accessed
July 19, 2017; www.latimes.com/entertainment/arts/culture/la-et-cm-diversity-arts-
study-devos-black-latino-groups-funding-20151009-story.html); Paul Reyes, 'Latinos
Speak Out about Lack of Diversity in NYC Arts, Culture Groups,' NBC News, February
2, 2016 (accessed July 21, 2017; www.nbcnews.com/news/latino/latinos-speak-out-
about-lack-diversity-nyc-arts-cultural-groups-n507451).

50. Australian Council for the Arts and Lateral Economics, *Arts Nation: An Overview of
Australian Arts Technical Appendix*, 2015 (Sydney: Australian Council for the Arts and
Lateral Economics, 2015; Accessed July 21, 2017; www.australiacouncil.gov.au/work-
space/uploads/files/research/arts-nation-technical-appendix-56382834062ea.pdf); Ien
Ang, 'The Predicament of Diversity: Multiculturalism in Practice at the Art Museum,'

Ethnicities 5 (3), 2005: 305-320; Andrew Taylor, 'Major Cultural Institutions Fail Workplace Diversity Targets,' *Sydney Morning Herald*, January 5, 2015 (accessed July 21, 2017; www.smh.com.au/entertainment/art-and-design/major-cultural-institutions-fail-workplace-diversity-targets-20150104-12fosn.html).

51. This is often out of our control, with the various gatekeepers, like school administrations, weighing in to block payment, often insisting that the children need to learn to value things other than money – easy for them to say.

52. ADD (attention deficit disorder) is the outdated term that has been replaced by ADHD, or attention deficit hyperactive disorder).

53. Recent examples include the Tate Modern and the Live Art Development Agency's launch of Sybille Peters' *Playing Up* project at the Tate (2016), the Leeds Beckett University's conference *With Children: The Child as Collaborator and Performer*; in Germany the performance company Skart and the Hamburg's Kampnagel Theatre's Masters of the Universe conference, Malmo's Moderna Museet's Basta Biennalen conference (2015), as well as a number of publications: Geesche Wartemann, Tülin Saglam, and Mary McAvoy, *Youth and Performance: Perceptions of the Contemporary Child* (New York: Georg Olms Verlag, 2015); G. Arrighi, V. Emeljanow, *Entertaining Children: The Participation of Youth in the Entertainment Industry* (London: Palgrave MacMillan, 2014); and Patrick Primavesi and Jan Deck, Jan, *Stop Teaching! Neue Theaterformen mit Kindern und Jugendlich* (London: Transcript Publishing House, 2014).

54. I'm currently in the process of attempting to see if the same principles can be applied in the context of the refugee crisis happening in Europe, with some positive results, as well as a different set of challenges. For more information: www.matchbox-rheinneckar.de/die-matches/detail/veranstaltung/ hemsbach-protocol-1/.

55. Chiapello Boltanski, *The New Spirit of Capitalism* (London: Verso Books, 2007).

56. See O'Donnell, *Social Acupuncture*, for more on the shortcomings of altruism as a force for sustainable social change.

57. Respectively, Marcel Duchamp's *Fountain* (1917), a readymade or found sculpture he used to test the openness of the newly created Society of Independent Artists in New York City; Damian Hirst's *The Physical Impossibility of Death in the Mind of Someone Living* (1991), a dead shark displayed in a vitrine floating in formaldehyde; and Jeanne van Heeswijk's *2Up2Down/ Homebaked* (2010), an urban planning initiative that resurrected a bakery, the success of the project expanding into an affordable housing scheme, community kitchen, and a land trust (for more information: www.2up2down. org.uk/).

58. Press Association, 'Coping with Risk and Danger Should Be Part of Curriculum – HSE Chair,' *Guardian*, March 27, 2016. www.theguardian.com/society/2016/ mar/27/coping-with-risk-and-danger-should-be-part-of-curriculum-hse-chair. Accessed July 22, 2017.

59. Leonore Skenazy, 'Update: Schools Advised to Install "Man Traps."' Free-Range Kids, March 2, 2017. Accessed July 29, 2017.

60. Pierre Bourdieu, *The Field of Cultural Production* (New York: Columbia University Press 1993): 31.

61. For a relentless litany of the wrongs done to children over the millennia, see Steven Pinker, *The Better Angels of Our Nature* (New York: Penguin Books, 2011).

62. Denise Foley, 'The Discipline Wars,' Time Inc. Accessed July 22, 2017. time.com/the-discipline-wars-2/. However, this list does not include the U.K., the U.S., Australia, or Canada, where much of Mammalian's work occurs. It is ironic that in some of these contexts, there is a prohibition against hugging, but violence remains on the table.

63. Pinker, *The Better Angels*: 444.

64. Lenore Skenazy, 'Court Sentences Dad to Hard Labor for Making His 8-Year-Old Son Walk a Mile as a Punishment,' *Reason*, January 13, 2017. Accessed July 22, 2017. reason.com/blog/2017/01/13/court-sentences-dad-to-hard-labor-for-ma; Tim Jones, Björn Frauendienst, Mayer Hillman, Andreas Redecker, Ben Shaw, and Ben Watson, 'Children's Independent Mobility in England and Germany (1971-2010)' (London: Policy Studies Institute, 2013). Accessed July 22, 2017. www.psi.org.uk/images/uploads/Briefing-Childrens_Independent_Mobility_v4_3.pdf.

65. Erin Brohmen, 'Winnipeg Mom Gets CFS Visit after Leaving Kids in Backyard to Play,' Canadian Broadcasting Corporation, April 29, 2016. Accessed July 22, 2017. www.cbc.ca/news/canada/manitoba/winnipeg-mom-cfs-backyard-play-children-1.3558471.

66. Mark Price, 'Free Preschool Given Playground Equipment, but Kids Can't Use It,' *Charlotte Observer*, October 23, 2016. Accessed July 22, 2017. www.charlotteobserver.com/news/local/article109691712.html.

67. Bridgette Dunlap, 'Why Prosecuting a Teen Girl for Sexting Is Absurd,' *Rolling Stone*, October 7, 2016. Accessed July 22, 2017. www.rollingstone.com/culture/news/why-prosecuting-a-teen-girl-for-sexting-is-absurd-w443829.

68. Hadley Freeman, '*Sesame Street*: Not Suitable for Children,' *Guardian*, November 26, 2007. Accessed July 22, 2017. www.theguardian.com/culture/tvandradioblog/2007/nov/26/sesamestreetnotsuitablefor.

69. Pinker, *The Better Angels*: 446.

70. French economist Thomas Piketty, in *Capital in the Twenty-First Century*, shows that when the rate of return on capital exceeds economic growth, the result is a rapid concentration of wealth in the hands of a minority. This was a hunch Marx had but did not have the data to substantiate.

71. For an example of this, subject yourself to this insufferable display of Warhol's tedious arrogance: wgbhstocksales, *Andy Warhol with Factory Interview*, YouTube video, 3:43 (September 1, 2009). Accessed July 22, 2017. youtu.be/ESGrKwldb8A.

72. Unless otherwise stated, all works were conceived and first directed by me.

73. The United Nations Committee on the Rights of the Child, 'Report on the forty-third session, Day of General Discussion on the Right to be Heard, Recommendations, Preamble' (Geneva: The United Nations, 2006).

74. Clarke Mackey's 2010 book *Random Acts of Culture* details the evolution of the role of the audience over the past several hundred years. He links the loss of public spaces filled with vibrant social connections with a corresponding change in the role of audience from one of active participant to one of passive spectator, from co-producer of cultural events to consumer. Cracks have begun to appear in the edifice with the rise of social and participatory aesthetics and technologies, but there are still many areas where participation is discouraged, particularly from children.

75. The United Nations Committee on the Rights of the Child, 'General Comment No. 1, The Aims of Education' (Geneva: The United Nations, 2001).

76. The United Nations Committee on the Rights of the Child, 'Report on the forty-third session.'

77. Ibid.

78. Rachel Hodgkin and Peter Newell, *Implementation Handbook for the Convention on the Rights of the Child* (New York: United Nations Children's Fund, 2007): 75.

79. The United Nations Committee on the Rights of the Child, 'General Comment No. 8, The right of the child to protection from corporal punishment and other cruel or degrading forms of punishment,' paragraphs 41, 43 (Geneva: The United Nations, 2006).

80. The United Nations Committee on the Rights of the Child, 'Sixth Session.'

81. The United Nations General Assembly, Universal Declaration of Human Rights, Article 19 (Paris: The United Nations, 1948).

82. Ibid.

83. The United Nations Committee on the Rights of the Child. 'General Comment No. 7, Implementing child rights in early childhood,' paragraph 5 (Geneva: The United Nations, 2006).

84. The United Nations General Assembly, 'Universal Declaration of Human Rights,' Article 19.

85. Hodgkin and Newell, *Implementation Handbook*: 154.

86. Ibid., 179

87. Ibid., 179.

88. Ibid., 180.

89. The United Nations. The United Nations Convention on the Rights of the Child, Article 13, paragraph 3 (Geneva: The United Nations, 1989).

90. The United Nations Committee on the Rights of the Child, 'General Comment No. 7.'

91. The United Nations. The United Nations Convention on the Rights of the Child, Article 5.

92. Hodgkin and Newell, *Implementation Handbook*: 181.

93. Ibid., 198.

94. Nico Trocmé and David Wolfe, *Child Maltreatment in Canada: Canadian Incidence Study of Reported Child Abuse and Neglect, Selected Results* (Ottawa: Minister of Public Works and Government Services Canada; Health Canada, 2001): 19.

95. Alister Lamont, *Who Abuses Children?* (Melbourne: Commonwealth of Australia, 2011); Don Grubin, *Sex Offending against Children: Understanding the risk* (London: Policing and Reducing Crime Unit Research, Development and Statistics Directorate Home Office, 1998); John A. Gaudiosi, *Child Maltreatment* (Washington: US Department of Health and Human Services, 2007).

96. Hodgkin and Newell, *Implementation Handbook*: 198.

97. Ibid.

98. The United Nations. The United Nations Convention on the Rights of the Child, Article 5.

99. Hodgkin and Newell, *Implementation Handbook*: 181.

100. Ibid., 198.

101. Trocmé and Wolfe, *Child Maltreatment in Canada*: 19.

102. Lamont, *Who Abuses Children?*; Grubin, *Sex Offending against Children*; Gaudiosi, *Child Maltreatment*.

103. Hodgkin and Newell, *Implementation Handbook*: 249.

104. The United Nations Committee on the Rights of the Child, 'General Comment No. 1, The Aims of Education.'

105. 'General Comment No. 13, The Right to Education,' paragraph 41 (Geneva: The United Nations, 1999): 71.

106. Hodgkin and Newell, *Implementation Handbook*: 262.

107. The United Nations Committee on the Rights of the Child, 'General Comment No. 8,' Section 3, paragraph 11.

108. Hodgkin and Newell, *Implementation Handbook*: 262.

109. The United Nations Committee on the Rights of the Child, 'Consideration of Report Submitted by State Parties,' Addendum 1, United Kingdom, paragraph 335 (Geneva: The United Nations, 1994).

110. Hodgkin and Newell, *Implementation Handbook*: 261.

111. The United Nations Committee on the Rights of the Child, 'General Comment No. 1, The Aims of Education,' paragraph 2.

112. The EPPI-Centre, *Understanding the Drivers, Impact and Value of Engagement in Culture and Sport*. (London: Department of Culture Media and Sport, 2010).

113. The United Nations Committee on the Rights of the Child, 'General Comment No. 1, The Aims of Education,' paragraph 2.

114. The United Nations Committee on the Rights of the Child, 'Report on the forty-third session.'

115. Ibid.

116. The United Nations Committee on the Rights of the Child, 'General Comment No. 1, The Aims of Education,' paragraph 8.

117. The United Nations Committee on the Rights of the Child, 'General Comment No. 8, The right of the child to protection from corporal punishment and other cruel or degrading forms of punishment,' Section 3, paragraph 11.

118. Hodgkin and Newell, *Implementation Handbook*: 455.

119. Louise Archer and Becky Francis, *Understanding Minority Achievement in Schools: Race, Gender, Class and 'Success'* (New York: Routledge, 2006).

120. Hodgkin and Newell, *Implementation Handbook*: 469.

121. International Association for the Child's Right to Play, Declaration of the Child's Right to Play (Malta, 1977). Accessed July 24, 2017. ipaworld.org/about-us/declaration/ipa-declaration-of-the-childs-right-to-play/.

122. Ibid.

123. Ibid.

124. Ibid.

125. The International Labour Organization, 'C138 Minimum Age Convention,' Article 6 (Geneva: The International Labour Organization, 1973).

126. The International Labour Organization. 'C060 Minimum Age (Non-Industrial Employ-ment) Convention,' Article 4 (Geneva: The International Labour Organization, 1932).

127. Hodgkin and Newell, *Implementation Handbook*: 544.

128. The United Nations Committee on the Rights of the Child, 'General Comment No. 7, Implementing Child's Rights in Early Childhood,' paragraph 36(e) (Geneva: The United Nations, 2005).

129. Hodgkin and Newell, *Implementation Handbook*: 544.

130. The United Nations, Conventions on the Rights of the Child, Article 29.1(d).

131. The United Nations Committee on the Rights of the Child, 'Report on the forty-third session.'

132. Ibid.

133. Hodgkin and Newell, *Implementation Handbook*: 445.

134. The United Nations Committee on the Rights of the Child, 'Report on the forty-third session.'

Works Cited

Ang, Ien. 'The Predicament of Diversity: Multiculturalism in Practice at the Art Museum.' *Ethnicities* 5, no. 3, 2005: 305-320.

Archer, Louise, and Becky Francis. *Understanding Minority Achievement in Schools: Race, Gender, Class and 'Success.'* New York: Routledge, 2006.

Australian Council for the Arts and Lateral Economics. *Arts Nation: An Overview of Australian Arts Technical Appendix, 2015.* Sydney: The Australian Council for the Arts and Lateral Economics, 2015 . Accessed July 21 , 2017 . www.australiacouncil.gov.au/ workspace/uploads/files/research/arts-nation-technical-appendix-56382834062ea.pdf.

Bedoya, Roberto. 'Considering Whiteness.' *Engaging Matters* (blog). The Arts Journal, February 20, 2016. Accessed July 19, 2017. www.artsjournal.com/engage/2013/02/ considering-whiteness.

Boehm, Mike. 'Study Sends "Wake-up Call" about Black and Latino Arts Groups' Meager Funding.' *Los Angeles Times*, October 12, 2015. Accessed July 19, 2017. www.latimes.com/ entertainment/arts/culture/la-et-cm-diversity-arts-study-devos-black-latino-groups-funding-20151009-story.html.

Boltanski, Luc, and Ève Chiapello. *The New Spirit of Capitalism.* Translated by Gregory Elliot. London, New York: Verso, 2007.

booba1234. 'David after Dentist.' YouTube Video, 1:28. January 30, 2009. Accessed July 17. 2017. youtu.be/txqiwrbYGrs.

Bourdieu, Pierre. *The Field of Cultural Production*, New York: Columbia University Press, 1993.

Bourriaud, Nicholas. *Relational Aesthetics.* Translated by Simon Pleasance and Fronza Woods. Dijon: Les Presses du Réel, 2002.

Brohmen, Erin. 'Winnipeg Mom Gets CFS Visit after Leaving Kids in Backyard to Play.' Canadian Broadcasting Corporation, April 29 , 2016 . Accessed July 22 , 2017 . www.cbc.ca/news/canada/manitoba/winnipeg-mom-cfs-backyard-play-children-1.3558471.

Brown, Stuart, and Christopher Vaughan. *Play: How It Shapes the Brain, Opens the Imagination, and Invigorates the Soul*, London: Penguin Books, 2009.

Butler, Tim, and Garry Robson. 'Social Capital, Gentrification and Neighbourhood Change in London: A Comparison of Three South London Neighbourhoods.' *Urban Studies*, 38, 12, 2001: 2145–2162.

The Cambridge Journal of Regions. 'Creatives after the Crash,' vol. 6, no. 1, 2013. Cambridge: Cambridge, The Cambridge Political Economy Society.

Ceci, Stephen J., and Wendy M. Williams. 'Schooling, Intelligence and Income.' *American Psychologist* 52, no. 10, 1997: 1051-1058.

Cooley, Alison, Amy Luo, and Caoimhe Morgan-Feir. 'Canada's Galleries Fall Short: The Not-So Great White North.' *Canadian Art*, April 21, 2015. Accessed July 19, 2017. canadianart.ca/features/canadas-galleries-fall-short-the-not-so-great-white-north/.

Curtis, Andy. *HyperNormalisation*, directed by Andy Curtis. London: BBC. 2016. Accessed July 17, 2017. www.bbc.co.uk/programmes/p04b183c.

Densham, Sophie. 'UK Game Market Soars Past £4.1 Billion.' Association for UK Interactive Entertainment, February 11, 2016. Accessed July 16, 2017. ukie.org.uk/node/29702

Dunlap, Bridgette. 'Why Prosecuting a Teen Girl for Sexting is Absurd.' *Rolling Stone*, October 7 , 2016 . Accessed July 22 , 2017 . www.rollingstone.com/culture/ news/why-prosecuting-a-teen-girl-for-sexting-is-absurd-w443829.

Durbin, Ben, et al. *The Impact of Creative Partnerships on School Attainment and Attendance.* Slough: National Foundation for Educational Research, 2010. Accessed July 17, 2012. www.creativitycultureeducation.org/wp-content/uploads/nfer-2010-impact-of-creative-partnerships-on-young-peoples-behavior-and-attainment-234.pdf.

Fineman, Martha Albertson. 'The Vulnerable Subject: Anchoring Equality in the Human Condition,' *Yale Journal of Law and Feminism* 20, no. 1, article 2, 2008.

Folbre, Nancy. *Valuing Children, Rethinking the Economics of the Family.* London: Harvard University Press. 2008.

Freeman, Hadley. 'Sesame Street: Not Suitable for Children.' *Guardian*, Novermber, 26, 2007. Accessed July 22 , 2017 . www.theguardian.com/culture/tvandradioblog/2007/nov/26/sesamestreetnotsuitablefor.

French, Michael T, Jenny F Homer, Ioana Popovici, Philip K. Robins. 'What You Do in High School Matters: High School GPA, Educational Attainment, and Labor Market Earnings as a Young Adult.' *Eastern Economic Journal*, 4, no. 3, 2015: 370-386.

Gaudiosi, John. A. *Child Maltreatment.* Washington: US Department of Health and Human Services, 2007.

Gray, Peter. 'The Decline of Play and the Rise of Psychopathology in Children and Adolescents.' *American Journal of Play*, 3, no. 4, 2011: 443-363.

Grubin, Don. *Sex Offending Against Children: Understanding the Risk.* London: Policing and Reducing Crime Unit Research, Development and Statistics Directorate Home Office, 1998.

Hill Strategies Research. *Mapping Artists and Cultural Working in Canada's Largest Cities.* Hamilton: Hill Strategies Research. February 9. 2010. Accessed July 17, 2017. www.hill-strategies.com/content/mapping-artists-and-cultural-workers-canada%E2%80%99s-large-cities2010.

Hodgkin, Rachel, and Peter Newell. *Implementation Handbook for the Convention on the Rights of the Child.* New York: United Nations Children's Fund, 2007.

International Labour Organization. 'C060 Minimum Age (Non-Industrial Employment) Convention.' Geneva: International Labour Organization, 1932.

———. 'C138 Minimum Age Convention.' Geneva: The International Labour Organization, 1973.

———. 'What Is Child Labour.' Accessed July 12, 2017. www.ilo.org/ipec/facts/lang--en/index.htm.

International Play Association. *Declaration of the Child's Right to Play.* Faringdon: International Play Association, 1977. Accessed July 23, 2017. Malta: International Play Association, 1979. ipaworld.org/childs-right-to-play/the-childs-right-to-play/.

Jones, Tim, Björn Frauendienst, Mayer Hillman, Andreas Redecker, Ben Shaw, Ben Watson. 'Children's Independent Mobility in England and Germany (1971-2010).' London: Policy Studies Institute, 2013. Accessed July 22, 2017. www.psi.org.uk/images/uploads/Briefing-Childrens_Independent_Mobility_v4_3.pdf.

Keller, Jared. 'The Psychological Case for Adult Play.' Accessed July 17, 2017. psmag.com/social-justice/throw-out-your-computer-and-grab-some-legos.

Kipps, Ben. 'How to Tie a Bow Tie for Dummies.' Youtube Video, 6:06. Posted May 13, 2012. youtu.be/ZoeNCvGbfYM.

Kirchofer, Dieter. 'The Reintegration of Children into the Adult World of Work: Ominous Sign or Cause for Optimism?' in *Working to Be Someone, Child Focused Research and Practice with Working Children*, ed. Beatrice Hungerland, Manfred Liebel, Brian Milne, Anne Wihstutz. London: Jessica Kingsley Publishers, 2007.

Lamont, Alister. *Who Abuses Children?* Melbourne: Commonwealth of Australia, 2011.

Mackey, Clarke. *Random Acts of Culture.* Toronto: Between the Lines, 2010.

Mazer, Katie, Katherine Rankin. 'The Social Space of Gentrification: The Politics of Neighbourhood Accessibility in Toronto's Downtown West.' *Environment and Planning D: Society and Space*, 29, 2011: 822- 839.

Newzoo. 'Top 100 Countries by Game Revenues.' Newzoo, June 2017. Accessed July 16, 2017. newzoo.com/insights/rankings/top-100-countries-by-game-revenues/.

O'Donnell, Darren. *Social Acupuncture: A Guide to Suicide, Performance and Utopia.* Toronto: Coach House Books, 2006.

Oldman, David. 'Childhood as a Mode of Production,' in *Children's Childhoods, Observed and Experienced*, edited by Berry Mayall, 153-166. London: The Falmer Press, 1994.

Pare, Mona. 'Inclusion and Participation in Special Education Processes in Ontario, Canada.' in *International Perspective and Empirical Findings on Child Participation*, edited by Tali Gal, 51-73. Oxford: Oxford University Press, 2015.

Pawson, Ray. *The Science of Evaluation: A Realist Manifesto.* London: Sage Publications, 2013.

Pew Research Center. *Teens, Social Media and Technology Overview 2015.* Washington: Pew Research Center, 2015. Accessed July 16, 2017. pewinternet.org/files/2015/04/PI_TeensandTech_Update2015_0409151.pdf.

Piketty, Thomas. *Capital in the Twenty First Century.* New York: Harvard University Press, 2014.

Press Association. 'Coping with Risk and Danger Should be Part of Curriculum – HSE Chair.' *Guardian*, March 27 , 2016 . Accessed July 22 , 2017 . www.theguardian.com/society/2016/mar/27/coping-with-risk-and-danger-should-be-part-of-curriculum-hse-chair.

Price, Mark. 'Free Preschool Given Playground Equipment, but Kids Can't Use It.' *Charlotte Observer*. October, 23 , 2016 . Accessed July 22 , 2017 . www.charlotteobserver.com/news/local/article109691712.html.

Primavesi, Patrick, and Jan Deck. *Stop Teaching! Neue Theaterformen mit Kindern und Jugendlich.* London: Transcript Publishing House, 2014.

Qvortup, Jens. 2001. 'School-work, Paid Work and the Changing Obligations of Childhood,' in *Future of Childhood: Hidden Hands: International Perspectives on Children's Work and Labour*, edited by Angela Bolton, Phillip Mizen, and Christopher Pole, 91-81. Abingdon, Oxon, US: Routledge, 2001.

Ramsay, Bob. 'Toronto Arts Boards in Dire Need of Diversity.' *Toronto Star*, June 10, 2015. Accessed July 19, 2017. www.thestar.com/opinion/commentary/ 2015/06/10/toronto-arts-boards-in-dire-need- of-diversity.html.

Reyes, Raul. 'Latinos Speak Out about Lack of Diversity in NYC Arts, Culture Groups.' NBC News, February 2 , 2016 . Accessed July 21 , 2017 . www.nbcnews.com/news/latino/latinos-speak-out-about-lack-diversity-nyc-arts-cultural-groups-n507451.

Rice, Zak Cheney. 'A Black Man Playing "Pokemon Go" Was Surrounded by Iowa City Officers with Guns Aimed at Him.' *Business Insider*, July 25, 2016. Accessed July 17, 2017. www.businessinsider.com/black-playing-pokemon-gochased-by-police-2016-7?IR=T.

Ridout, Nicholas. 'Performance in the Service Economy: Outsourcing and Delegation,' in *Double Agent*, edited by Claire Bishop and Silvia Tramontana. London: Institute of Contemporary Arts, 2009.

Sack, Sally. Foreword to *What Is Art: Conversations with Joseph Beuys*, edited by Volker Harlan. Forest Row: Clairview, 2012.

Scott, Allen, J. 'Creative Cities: Conceptual Issues and Policy Questions.' *Journal of Urban Affairs* 28, no. 1, 2006: 1–17.

Skenazy, Lenore. 'Court Sentences Dad to Hard Labor for Making His 8-Year-Old Son Walk a Mile as a Punishment.' *Reason*, January 13, 2017. Accessed July 22, 2017. reason.com/blog/2017/01/13/court-sentences-dad-to-hard-labor-for-ma.

———. 'Update: Schools Advised to Install "Man Traps."' *Free-Range Kids*, March 2, 2017. Accessed July 29, 2017. www.freerangekids.com/schools-advised-to-install-man-traps/.

Stuart, Cameron, and Jon Coaffee. 'Art, Gentrification and Regeneration: From Artist as Pioneer to Public Arts.' *European Journal of Housing Policy*, 5, no. 1, 2005: 39–58.

Taylor, Andrew. 'Major Cultural Institutions Fail Workplace Diversity Targets.' *Sydney Morning Herald*, January 5, 2015. Accessed July 21, 2017. www.smh.com. au/entertainment/art-and-design/major-cultural-institutions-fail-workplace-diversity-targets-20150104-12fosn.html.

Trocmé, Nico. Wolfe, David. *Child Maltreatment in Canada: Canadian Incidence Study of Reported Child Abuse and Neglect, Selected Results*. Ottawa: Minister of Public Works and Government Services Canada; Health Canada, 2001.

United Nations. *The International Covenant on Civil and Political Rights*. New York: The United Nations, 1966. www.ohchr.org/EN/ProfessionalInterest/Pages/ CCPR.aspx.

———. *The United Nations Convention on the Rights of the Child*. Geneva: The United Nations, 1989. .www.ohchr.org/EN/ProfessionalInterest/Pages/ CRC.aspx.

———. *The Universal Declaration of Human Rights*. New York: The United Nations, 1948. www.un.org/en/universal-declaration-human-rights/.

United Nations Committee on Economic, Social and Cultural Rights. 'General Comment No. 13, The Right to Education.' Geneva: The United Nations, 1999.

United Nations Committee on the Rights of the Child. 'Consideration of Report Submitted by State Parties,' Addendum 1, United Kingdom, paragraph 335. Geneva: The United Nations, 1994.

———. 'General Comment No. 1, The Aims of Education.' Geneva: United Nations, 2001.

———. 'General Comment No. 7: Implementing Child's Rights in Early Childhood.' Geneva: The United Nations, 2005.

———. 'General Comment No. 8: The Right of the Child to Protection from Corporal Punishment and Other Cruel or Degrading Forms of Punishment.' Geneva: The United Nations, 2006.

———. 'Report on the Forty-Third Session, Day of General Discussion on the Right to be Heard,' recommendations, preamble, September 29, 2006.

———. 'Report on the Twenty-Eighth Session.' Geneva: The United Nation, 2001.

Wartemann, Geesche, Tülin Saglam, and Mary McAvoy. *Youth and Performance: Perceptions of the Contemporary Child*, Medien Und Theater. New York: Georg Olms Verlag, 2015.

The Warwick Commission. *Enriching Britain: Culture, Creativity and Growth: The 2015 Report by the Warwick Commission on the Future of Cultural Value*. Coventry: The University of Warwick, 2015. Accessed July 19, 2017. www2.warwick.ac.uk/research/warwickcommission/futureculture/finalreport/.

Watson, Alison M. *The Child in International Politics: A Place at the Table*. London: Routledge, 2009.

wgbhstocksales. 'Andy Warhol with Factory Interview.' YouTube video, 3:43. September 1, 2009. Accessed July 22, 2017. youtu.be/ESGrKwldb8A.

Wihstutz, Anne. 'The Significance of Care and Domestic Work to Children: A German Portrayal, in *Working to Be Someone: Child Focused Research and Practice with Working Children*, ed. Beatrice Hungerland, Manfred Liebel, Brian Milne, and Anne Wihstutz, 77-86. London: Jessica Kingsley Publishers, 2007.

Wright, Robin, Lindsay John, and Julia Sheel. 'Lessons Learned from the National Arts and Youth Demonstration Project.' *Journal of Children and Family Studies*, volume 16, no. 1, 2007: 48-58.

Zukin, Sharon. 'Gentrification: Culture and Capital in the Urban Core.' *Annual Review of Sociology*, 3, 1987): 129-137.

ACKNOWLEDGEMENTS

I'm especially indebted to producer Naomi Campbell, my first Mammalian partner, who built the infrastructure of the company from scratch, co-developed *Haircuts by Children*, and took it on the road with me for the first few iterations. She introduced the project to Steve Ball, from Birmingham's Fierce Festival, who passed it to his brother and festival director Mark Ball, who presented our European premiere. Thanks to the Brothers Ball.

A big shout-out also goes out to Ernie Bolton, the principal at Parkdale Public School, who first granted us access to the students, with the very steely question *What's in it for the kids?* Joe Leibovitch, our point person at the school for *Parkdale Public School vs. Queen Street West*, was also a great ally, as were many of the other staff members, including Carolyn Wallace, Amanda Biber, Sandra Hamilton, and Sandra De Angelis.

A lot of great additional insights have been derived through our collaboration with the Ruhrtriennale Festival, which was triggered by Marietta Piekenbrock, first under the direction of Heiner Goebbels, then Johan Simons. Ruhrtriennale dramaturge Cathrin Rose, her staff, and German Mammalian Jana Eiting, who has worked with us constantly since then, and Cathrin's whole family – Christian Meyer, Emma, Jonathan, and Valentine – have all become great friends over the years. Cathrin embodies the ideas in this book, and we've had many great conversations about the role of children in world in general and in the performing arts in particular. The Ruhrtriennale offered the unusual opportunity to work with the same group of children since 2012, something I've only been able to previously do with the Toronto youth.

Mark Ball gets a second shout-out with his team at the London International Festival Theatre (LIFT): Beki Bateson, Erica Campanye, Patricia Akoli, Bonnie Green, and Francis Christeller. A big nod goes to producer Selma Nichols for her role in guiding the project in its first year, as well as the artists who are on the front line of the project: Elsabet Yonas, Güneş Güvenify, Imwen Eke, Jeremy Carne, Jessica Murrain, Kazuko Hohki, Keren Ghitis, Louis Parker-Evans, and Theodora Omambala. LIFT is engaged in the first deliberate replication of the model outlined in the chapter 'Children vs. Mammalian Diving Reflex' and developed in collaboration with the Toronto youth. We are working with the children at the Northumberland Park Community School and the Vale School over the course of five years, 2015 to 2020.

This long-term project was designed by me, co-directed with Alice Fleming, and supported by the great staff at both schools, including head teacher Monica Duncan and her team: Diane Liversidge, Jenny Baily, and Kayleigh Lloyd, and, from the Vale School, deputy head Tony Millard, with receptionist Maureen Lee-Hixon always bringing the party.

Roya Amirsoleymani, Angela Mattox, Victoria Frey, and their staff at the Portland Institute of Contemporary Art have also facilitated a number of the book's insights by hiring me to study the possibility of developing a youth engagement strategy for the PICA through the Doris Duke Foundation. Harrell Fletcher, Lisa Jarrett, and their brilliant grad students at the Portland State University's Social Practice program have been super-supportive and the source of many great conversations.

Paula Poletto, Judy Koke, Kathleen McClean, and Syrus Ware at the Art Gallery of Ontario, as well many of the directors of the gallery's departments, were very helpful during Mammalian's residency, where I examined the possibility of applying these ideas in a large institutional setting, in collaboration with members of the Youth Council.

Some of these ideas were first presented in the *Humber Review*, edited by the ever-supportive and encouraging Sarah Armenia.

Generously providing critical feedback on early drafts of this book were Alice Fleming, Rochelle Hum, Tina Fance, Annalise Prodor, Sijia Li, Tony Millard, Kelly O'Donnell, Lianne O'Donnell, Troy O'Donnell, Sibylle Peters, and, in particular, Susan Sheddan, Convener of Tate's Early Years and Family in London, who provided detailed feedback and plenty of debate about the points raised here.

I direct a wave of pure adulation toward editor Alana Wilcox at Coach House Books, and publisher Stan Bevington, the man you see on the cover nervously getting his hair cut, as well as Norman Nehmetallah and Jessica Rattray, and John De Jesus and his crew in the bindery. A big hug to John Lauener, the photographer responsible for the iconic photo on the cover, as well as Amahays Mulugeta and Dailia Linton, who are making Stan look so nervous.

Also big, big love with maple syrup on top to all of the interns, observers, board members, and staff who have churned through Mammalian over the years, keeping things rolling on the home front, even as it is the most unusual and least professional environment on the planet, and unlikely to change anytime soon. A special nod goes out to board member Sean Craig, who actually took the time to be friends with the youth, in addition to helping us move. Anyone who is willing to carry a filing cabinet up flights of stairs is a friend for life.

Kalpna Patel and Anupa Khemadasa Perera deserve a hearty slap on the back for all the time they spend with me and the youth in Toronto, including the times we spent making work together. Lenine Bourke, who co-developed *These Are the People in Your Neighbourhood*, is an especially valued friend and collaborator, and we've had a lot of great conversations about working with children. A very special creative thanks goes out to one of my all-time favourite collaborators, filmmaker Nicole Bazuin, who worked with the youth and me on our film projects, easily some of the best work we've made. Thanks also to Jenna Winter, who was Mammalian's managing director (2010–2016) and was central to keeping the whole operation on track as we worked in Parkdale and around the world.

Though mentioned in the dedication, it is worth emphasizing here the absolutely central role of Eva Verity. In addition to dealing with all the project's logistics, fighting for bigger budgets, and making sure the hair salons are beautiful, she directs many of the touring projects, enduring near-continuous jet lag and the many challenges bundled with collaborating with children, and sharing her many insights. Without Eva, there is no Mammalian.

Finally, an incredible thanks to the thousands of children and young people Mammalian has worked with over the years, as well as the many schools and other institutions that have collaborated with us, a big list that keeps on growing and will be out of date before this is published: Adelaide's Blair Athol North Primary School and learning advisors Nathan Anderson, Marta Cichonski, Penny Cook, Concetta De Leo, Shohreh Fallah, Debbie Grose, David Gross, Stephanie Hentschel, Kylie McRostie, Daniel Niyonkuru, and Carolyn Sugars; Austin's Pecan Springs Elementary School and school facilitator Starla Simmons; Birmingham Repertory Theatre and Birmingham's Wheelers Lane Technology College and teacher Emma Vaughan; Bologna's Scuola Elementary School and teacher Giovanna Del Vitto; Bochum's Erich Kästner-Schule and teachers Marianne Heemskerk and Jörg Heinemann; Brussels's Ecole Aurore, Vier Winden, and Lutgardisschool and teachers Karlien Tiebout, Wim Van de Brulle, and Isabelle Warzee; Copenhagen's Sønderbro School and teachers Malene Christiansen and Klaus Vestergaard; Cork's St. Vincent's Primary School and principal Marie Ni Eiki and teacher Lesley-Ann, and Cork's North Presentation Primary School's principal Kathleen Haverty and teachers Laura Mitchell and Nollaig Cleary; Darwin's Millner Primary School and teachers Sheree Arratta and Jackie Haines; Derry, Ireland's Oakgrove Integrated Primary School and principal Ann

Murray; Dublin's St. Joseph's Primary School and Ms. White and Mr. O'hici; teachers at Duisburg's Gesamtschule Globus am Dellplatz and Herbert Grillo Gesamtschule, Essen's Parkschule, and Gelsenkirchen's Gesamtschule Ückendorf; Ghent's Freinetschool Mandala and teachers Nina Leroy, Barbara Vlaeminck, and facilitator Liesa Vandenhende; Gladbeck's Erich Kästner-Realschule and teacher Barbora Granderath; Glasgow's Oak Grove Primary School; teachers at Gwangju's Dongsan Elementary School; Hamilton Artists Inc., arts group NgeN and facilitator Simon Orpana; Kitchener-Waterloo's Suddaby Public School and teachers Trevor Davies and Tanya Hofman; Kuopio's Ala-Pyörö School and teacher Anja Siltakoski; Launceston, Tasmania's Mowbray Heights Primary and teachers Marcella Glachan, Karen Higgens, Judy Harris, Chris Cullen, Kathy Robson, and Julia Rodwell; Lahore's Punjabi Lok Mela and Shafiq Butt; London's community of Canning Town and Newham; Los Angeles's Burbank Middle School; Manchester's Abandon Normal Devices and coordinators Neil Winterburn and Marisa Draper; Manhattan's Dr. Sun Yat Sen School and teachers Ms. Moulinos and Ms. Hodges; Melbourne's Footscray Arts Centre; Montreal's Westmount Park School and teachers Ms. Hope, Mr Noah, and Ms. Jody Wilson; Mumbai's Aarambh and Shobha Murthi; Mullheim an der Ruhr's Willy Brandt Schule; Newcastle-upon-Tyne's Walkergate Primary School; Norwich's Catton Grove Primary School and teachers Agnes Pattison and Dan McKeown, and City Academy Norwich and teacher Duncan Joseph; Oldenburg's Hauptschule Kreyenbrück and teachers Ute Knaab and Tomke Janssen; Prague's ZS Brána jazyku and teachers Alena Cižinská, Hana Novotná, and Sylva Bartakovicová; Toronto's Parkdale Public School and principal James Smyth, teachers Amanda Biber, Carolyn Wallace, Sandra De Angelis, Sandra Hamilton, and the entire staff; Fairbank Middle School, Dovercourt Junior Primary School, and teachers Fiona Brougham and Lisa Furdyk; Duke of Connaught Junior and Senior Public School and teacher Effie Ko; Lord Dufferin Junior and Senior Public School and Shelly Lowry; George Peck Public School; R. H. McGregor Elementary School and teacher Pam Jen; Rose Avenue Junior Public School and teacher Sandra Fisher; Toronto's Just BGRAPHIC, Urban Arts, Theatre for Peace, Art Starts, and Arts for Children and Youth; Perth, Australia's Roseworth Primary School; Portland's Glenfair Elementary School and Ms. Rosineau; Regina's Davin School and teacher Kelly Maupin and principal Loraine O'Donnell, and Regina's Arcola Community School and teacher Danielle Dumelie; Surrey, Canada's Bridgeview Elementary, principal Judy Gram and teachers Jeanne Atwal,

Elizabeth Hinman, Ms. MacKenzie, and Ms. Ens, and principal Andrew Shook and teacher Omar Obdollal; Terni's Scuole Elementari Manzolini and teacher Marcella Grandoni; Victoria's George Jay Elementary School and Mrs. Belanger; and Whitehorse's Elijah Smith Elementary School and teacher Robyn Murphy.

Darren O'Donnell is an urban cultural planner, novelist, essayist, playwright, director, and filmmaker. He is the artistic director of performance company Mammalian Diving Reflex and research director of Methods for Mammals. He holds a BFA in theatre, a MSc in urban planning from the University of Toronto, and studied traditional Chinese and Western medicine at the Shiatsu School of Canada. His books include *Social Acupuncture*, which argues for aesthetics of civic engagement, and *Your Secrets Sleep with Me*, a novel about difference, love, and the miraculous. His stage-based works include *All the Sex I've Ever Had*, *The Hemsbach Protocol*, *Promises to a Divided City*, *A Suicide-Site Guide to the City*, *White Mice*, and *[boxhead]*. His performance works include *Haircuts by Children*, *Nightwalks with Teenagers*, *Eat the Street*, and *The Children's Choice Awards*. His films include *High School Health*, *Sleeping with Family*, *Allegations*, and *How to Be a Brown Teen*. His urban cultural planning clients include the Tate Modern; the London International Festival of Theatre; the Portland Institute for Contemporary Art; the Metropolitan Region of Rhine-Neckar, Germany; and the West Kowloon Cultural District, Hong Kong. He currently lives out of a suitcase, primarily dividing his time between Europe, the U.K., Australia, and Canada.

To get in touch: darren@mammalian.ca.

Typeset in Aragon, Aragon Sans, and Mirador.

Printed at the Coach House on bpNichol Lane in Toronto, Ontario, on Rolland Opaque Natural paper, which was manufactured, acid-free, in Saint-Jérôme, Quebec, from 50 percent recycled paper, and it was printed with vegetable-based ink on a 1973 Heidelberg KORD offset litho press. Its pages were folded on a Baumfolder, gathered by hand, bound on a Sulby Auto-Minabinda, and trimmed on a Polar single-knife cutter.

Edited by Alana Wilcox
Cover design by Ingrid Paulson
Cover photograph by John Lauener

Coach House Books
80 bpNichol Lane
Toronto ON M5S 3J4
Canada

416 979 2217
800 367 6360

mail@chbooks.com
www.chbooks.com